Sculpting Cane Handles

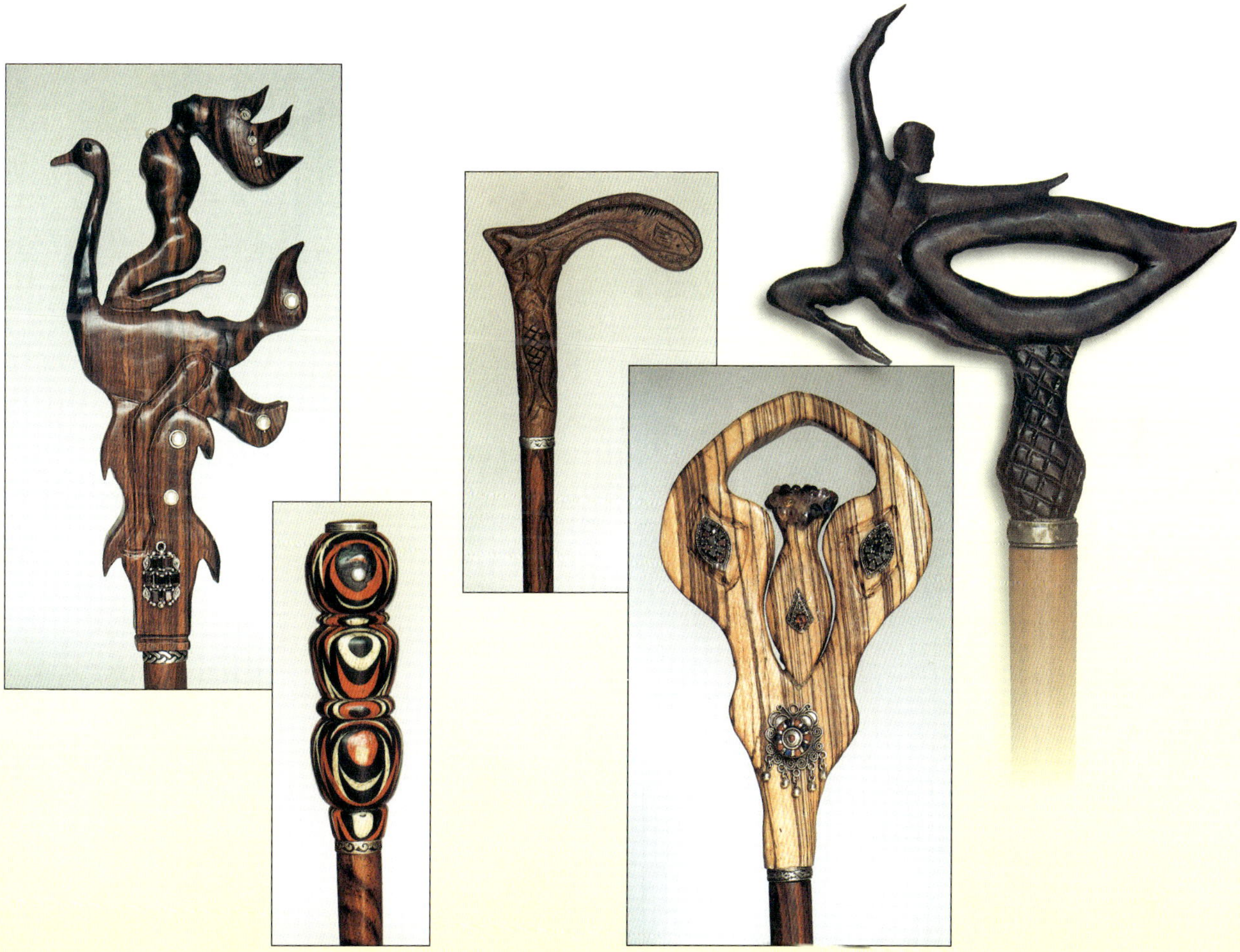

Nicolo Scariano

Schiffer Publishing Ltd®

4880 Lower Valley Road, Atglen, Pennsylvania 19310

Dedication

Dedicated to the memory of my best friend, Giuseppe Amoroso, who in Italy saved and returned to me my grandfather's cane, which sparked the idea of making cane handles and then this book. Also to Nicholas, Joseph, Christopher, Patrick, Andrew, Marc, Lauren, Matthew, William, my grandchildren... and their parents.

Photograph of author credit: Fred Guarinello
All other photographs: Nicolo Scariano

Other Schiffer Books on Related Subjects

86 Cane Patterns for the Woodcarver. Tom Wolfe.
Canes & Walking Sticks. Jeffrey B. Snyder.
Canes From the Seventeenth to the Twentieth Century. Jeffrey B. Snyder.
Canes Through the Ages. Francis H. Monek.
Carving Animal Canes & Walking Sticks with Power. Frank C. Russell.
Carving Fancy Walking Sticks. Tom Wolfe.
Carving Wildfowl Canes and Walking Sticks with Power. Frank C. Russell.
Router Canes. Dale Power.
Walkingsticks. Ulrick Klever.

Library of Congress Control Number: 2007942555

Designed by Mark David Bowyer
Type set in Arrus BT / Zurich BT

ISBN: 978-0-7643-2823-7
Printed in China

Published by Schiffer Publishing Ltd.
4880 Lower Valley Road
Atglen, PA 19310
Phone: (610) 593-1777; Fax: (610) 593-2002
E-mail: Info@schifferbooks.com

In Europe, Schiffer books are distributed by
Bushwood Books
6 Marksbury Ave.
Kew Gardens
Surrey TW9 4JF England
Phone: 44 (0) 20 8392-8585; Fax: 44 (0) 20 8392-9876
E-mail: info@bushwoodbooks.co.uk
Website: www.bushwoodbooks.co.uk
Free postage in the U.K., Europe; air mail at cost.

Contents

Acknowledgments

My gratitude to my wife, Jean, who helped in the composition and computer work and to Rosemarie Paternostro who advised on the first draft. Also to Mr. Jeffrey Snyder, my editor, who gave me an understanding of the expertise needed by an editor in the world of publishing.

Introduction

New Ideas

The following pages contain a collection of handmade canes. This is not a collection of canes made by various people from different parts of the world or during various periods of history. Rather, these are all canes created by the author.

This book is addressed to wood lovers, cane lovers, cane makers, and cane collectors. It is not designed for commercial reasons but is an expression of the love and joy the author experiences while creating his unique cane handles.

The canes in this book were designed by and executed within a two year period. The handles of these canes reflect the author's vision and artistic talents. This book does not address carving the shafts of the canes.

Making Canes

The Shaft

Today, very little attention is given to the shaft. In fact, many commercially made shafts go so far as to misrepresent the material used in the shaft. A shaft sold as ebony may well be ebonized – that is – wood painted black and lacquered. In my case, all my shafts are made from natural hardwoods.

Upon completion of a cane handle, the specifications for a shaft are sent to an artisan in Costa Rica. The shafts are made with beautiful, exotic hardwoods such as cocobola (*Dalbergia Refusa*), Ron-Ron (*Astronium Graveolerns*), Mara wood (*Fustic*), and ironwood (*Gualycon Real*). The hardwood for each shaft is selected to complement the materials and artistry of the cane handle.

The Handle

The cane handle is the most important part of the cane. It is in the cane handle where one can exercise creativity. Any form, shape or color may be adapted into a handle. Being a physician and a lover of nature, it is natural that the female body is my most frequently used subject. However, animals and birds are also excellent subjects for the cane handle. Animal lovers, such as dog and horse lovers are excellent recipients for cane handles that depict their favorite animals.

The Shape of the Cane Handles

The most common, conventional shapes used in the construction of the handles are the knob, crook, and opera or "T" shapes. Usually, the user's hand grasps the sculpture. I wanted to break with tradition and experimented with an unconventional shape that I call the "lip shape" or "mouth shape" and the "double-deck shape." Frequently, the sculptures that I create are one piece with the lip handle. The hand does not grasp the sculpture; it grasps only the "Lip."

All handles should be anatomically correct and beautiful. At times, it is necessary to have artistry prevail over anatomy. However, it is most important that the user of the cane should have a continuous feeling of joy and admiration for the cane handle.

The Selection of Materials for the Cane Handles

Most of my cane handles, except for those in Colorplay wood or holly wood, are made from exotic woods. The woods I use most often are Macassar ebony, zebrawood, rosewood, purple heart, and holly wood, I did experiment with woods from Sicily but found them unsuitable for this type of sculpture. I prefer wood rather than metal. Wood has a natural grain that enhances the beauty and richness of the sculpture.

The use of a combination of woods in the making of cane handles is an option open to artists, based on their goals and discretion. It is very natural and appealing to me to combine two woods: ebony (the darkest wood in nature) with holly wood (the lightest wood in nature). Both are ideal for sculpturing because both woods are very appealing to the eye.

Sculpturing the Handles: Techniques

Every sculpture begins with an idea in your mind. Ideas can come from living things, previous sculptures, art books, sports books, and newspapers.

Once the idea is firmly set in my mind, the next step is to sketch the handle on paper. The sketching of a cane handle is a long and arduous process for me.

Once I am satisfied with the design (drawing), I must next consider the type(s) of wood(s) I want to use and then match the grain with the sketch. The drawing is then glued onto the wood and the contour is cut using a band saw.

The cut sculpture is worked on the round with a rotary tool. Now, the piece is ready for the long, tedious process of sanding and spraying. I start with 80 grade sandpaper and progress to 240 grade sandpaper. A satin lacquer spray is applied to the wood. A hole is drilled at the base of the handle. Before the handle is attached, the silver ring or collar is placed at the base of the handle. The custom-made shaft has a 3" to 4" long screw already attached and it is screwed into the handle of the cane and the cane collar is fitted to hide the connection and to add decoration.

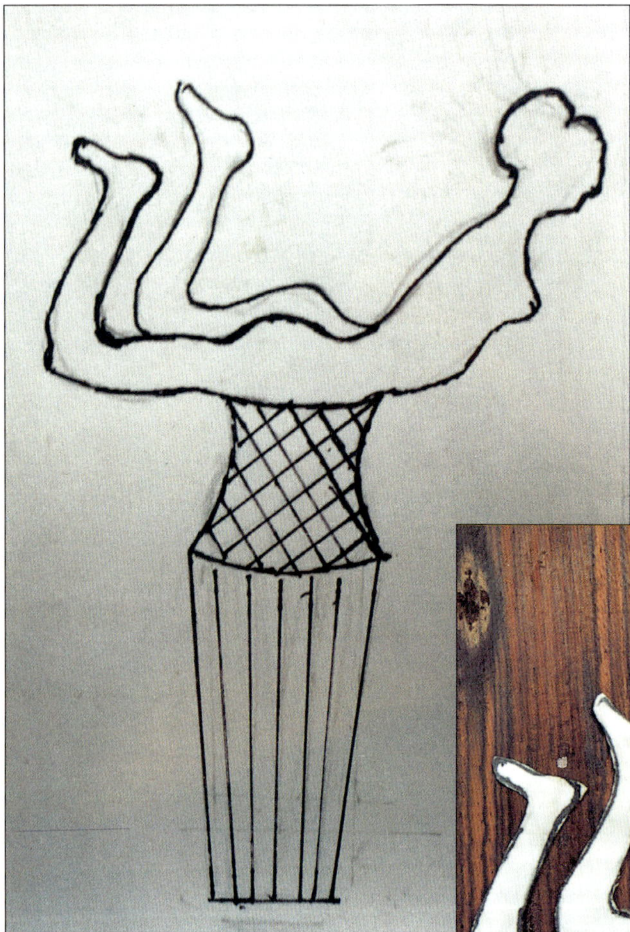

The design is on traceable paper.

The design is attached to the wood.

The sculpture after being cut with a band saw.

The sculpture is sketched using chalk for marking the details.

A hole is drilled at the base of the sculpture.

The handle is attached to the shaft with a long screw, with the insertion of a silver collar at the point of attachment.

The complete, finished sculpture.

Some silver rings.

Colorplay™ Wood

I remembered that I had a few blocks of Colorplay wood, which I had acquired a few years back. Colorplay wood is a stained laminated wood compressed in a special process. The blocks of wood, made in Italy, come in different colors. The blocks can be cut and placed in a lathe. When I placed them on the lathe, I obtained a beautiful kaleidoscopic pattern that is different for each block. I started sketching the profile of the handles and made a template that I used while turning the piece.

Mixing of Woods of Different Colors

What follows is useful advice about combining different woods in different colors and grains. The first two photographs in the series show the meaning of the word "orchid." It is a derivative of the Greek word *"orchis,"* meaning genitalia. The word was given to these flowers for the strange resemblance of many of these flowers to the male and female anatomy. In the construction of these handles, I assembled different species of wood in different colors, grain, and thickness together with Colorplay wood.

I have previously, briefly touched upon the technique I used to assemble sculptures composed of different varieties of wood. In discussing the sculpting of the present series, I will try to include finer details of my technique for creating sculptures composed of different varieties of wood so that readers will have a better understanding of the process.

In choosing a variety of wood, I pay attention to the thickness of the piece. The upper part of the handle, the part which is grasped with the palm of the hand, requires a thickness of approximately one to one and a half inches, while the lower part of the handle, where the sculpture is located using the human form or a bird will require a piece of wood thicker by approximately two to three inches in order to create a three-dimensional sculpture.

I start drawing each piece on tracing paper. Each handle is composed of three to five pieces of different varieties of wood. Color, grain, and thickness are carefully selected. Then the three to five components of the handle are separated on paper and each component, on paper, is glued to a previously chosen variety of wood.

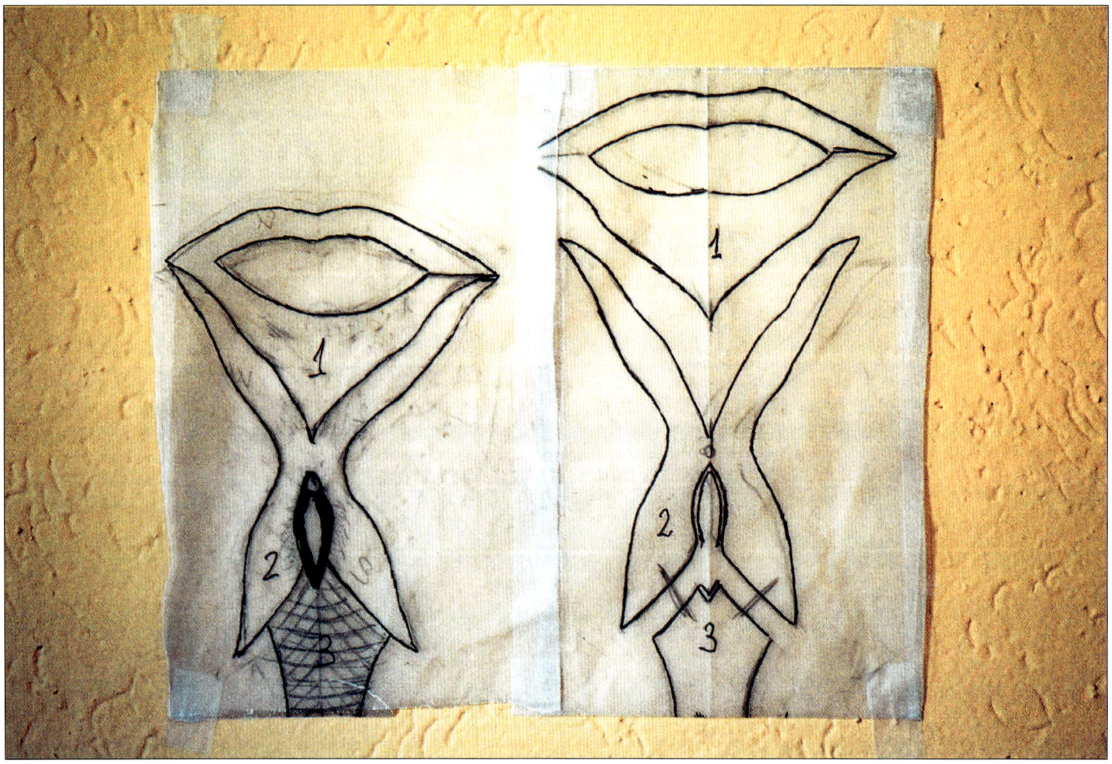

The wood is then cut using a 14" band saw with a narrow blade made for hard wood.

The three to five pieces of the cut wood are worked "in the round" with rotary tools and then re-united with regular wood glue or a two-part glue. **A two-part glue is comprised of resin and a hardener. There are two separate bottles. This glue requires precise mixing according to the instructions for optimum bonding. I use System 3™.** If necessary, the joints are reinforced with wood dowels or steel expansion rods.

The handle is reconstructed again in this way.

When necessary in order to hide the joints, I make a paste by mixing wood glue with the wood powder of the same wood with which I am working. I collect the clean part of the wood powder resulting from use of the band saw and rotary tools. Once the joint filler is set, the reassembled handle is worked again "in the round" with rotary tools, cleaned, and sanded with 80, 120, and 240 grain sanding paper in that order. I clean the sanded handle by using steel wool and then a fine brush. The base of the handle is then rounded using rotary tools in order to achieve a diameter equal to the diameter of the shaft. A hole is drilled in the center using a hole saw bit to accommodate the silver ring and the 3" - 4" wood screw of the shaft. The final step requires spraying with several coats of primer and flat or satin clear lacquer spray.

Abstract of an orchid composed of three different woods: Brazilian rosewood, ebony, and tulipwood. 9 x 5 inches. Silver connecting ring. Pink and red hard stones ornament the two faces of the sculpture.

The complete handle is adorned with gemstones. The location where the stone will be attached is chosen. Size, color, and peculiarities of the stone are considered to match the color and the grain of the wood. The gemstone is attached to the wood with small nails, pins, and two-part glue. The jewelry is covered with tape and the sculpture is sprayed again with clear lacquer spray.

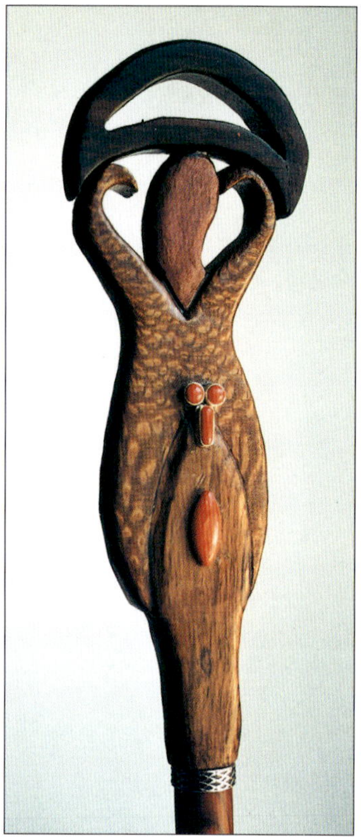

Abstract of an orchid composed of four different woods: Macassar ebony, Purple Heart, lacewood, Honduras Rose Wood. 11 x 4 inches. Silver connecting ring. Red stones on one side and white stones on the opposite face adorn the sculpture.

When the handle is completed and the stones attached, the handle is ready to be photographed. I use a non-digital camera with a 105-135 lens and Kodachrome™ film, using natural light from a window, and – most of the time – a white background.

Shows a woman located inside the handle and in the same axel of the shaft. The sculpture is composed of four different woods: Tulip, ebony, Colorplay, and Macassar rosewood. 12 x 4 inches. Silver connecting ring.

This handle has a peculiar feature. The center of the carving, a woman with a long skirt in Colorplay, is located inside the handle and in the same axel of the shaft. The sculpture is composed of five different woods: Lace, Costa Rica cocobola, Colorplay, zebra, and holly. 10 x 4 inches. Silver connecting ring.

A clown with facial features made with small stones composed of four different woods: Macassar ebony, Tulip, Colorplay, and rosewood. 8 x 4 inches. Silver connecting ring.

The Connecting Ring or Collar

The connecting ring serves the purpose of hiding the joint between the shaft and the handle. The first connectors that I made were of bronze (one to two inches long) that were corrugated with rotary tools. Later, I embraced the idea of using single or double silver rings made in India and Italy.

The Ferrule

The ferrule is very often a forgotten part of the cane. Most commercially made canes do not use a ferrule, but opt for an inexpensive tip composed of plastic or rubber. Without a ferrule, the cane appears unfinished. The ferrule is designed to protect the shaft and give stability to the cane. Many of my ferrules are made from bone, metal, or plastic.

A metal ferrule gives the best appearance and is long lasting. However, most metal ferrules can also be slippery. I prefer to use plastic or bull horn and cover with a rubber tip.

Most of my ferrules are done individually to afford me the opportunity to decorate the ferrule and make an artistic connection to the shaft.

The plastic, Teflon™ rods that I use are black or white and have a high degree of hardness and high melting points. The Teflon rods are cut in sections of one, two or three inches. A hole is drilled in one end of the rod and a brass screw is inserted in the hole.

The Ferrule: Technique

A regular lathe holds both extremities of the piece to be turned. But I choose to use a standard rotary tool with a chuck that holds only one end. This is possible by turning only small pieces – one to two inches in length. Most of the metal ferrules that are used are hollow and banged. My Teflon ferrules are solid. They are attached to the shaft with bronze screws. The screw, along with the rod, is inserted in the chuck of the rotary motor that I use as a lathe. The rod is given a tapered shape and decorated with circular rings.

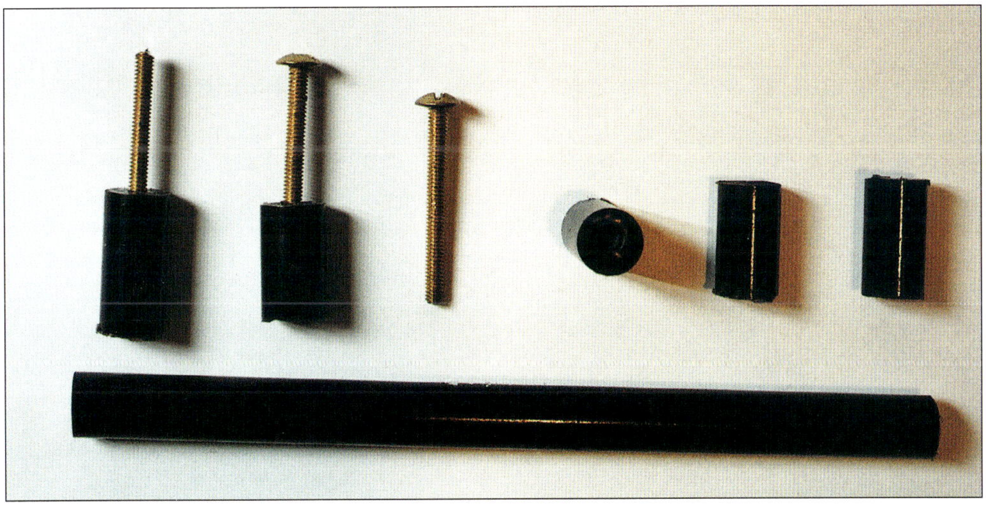

Sections of rods in hard Teflon and hard Buffalo Horn, some with brass screws attached.

Ferrules with a screw attached.

Turning the ferrule on a regular drill.

Finished ferrule in hard plastic or Buffalo Horn.

Finishing Touches – Hard Stones

During the summer months, the beaches of Sicily are crowded with tourists and vendors. These vendors are selling gemstones and costume jewelry that was manufactured in India and Pakistan. The idea occurred to me to add these gemstones to my canes.

However, I soon realized that the best way to apply the stones was to make handles that were predisposed to having gemstones inserted.

Cane Holders

After I had made more then one hundred canes, I realized that I needed a stable stand to support and display the collection. Earlier I had designed and built a wooden stand with eighteen burr holes to accommodate the first completed canes. I then needed a stand to support and display forty canes and designed and built a stand on two levels to hold fifty canes. Finally, I built three floor models with fluted holes to accommodate five, twenty, and thirty canes.

Finished ferrule in hard plastic or Buffalo Horn.

Handle Types

Simple Handles of Abstract Birds Made With One Inch Zebrawood

Abstract of a bird: the grain of the wood is obliquely placed; handle size is six inches by six inches with brass corrugated collar.

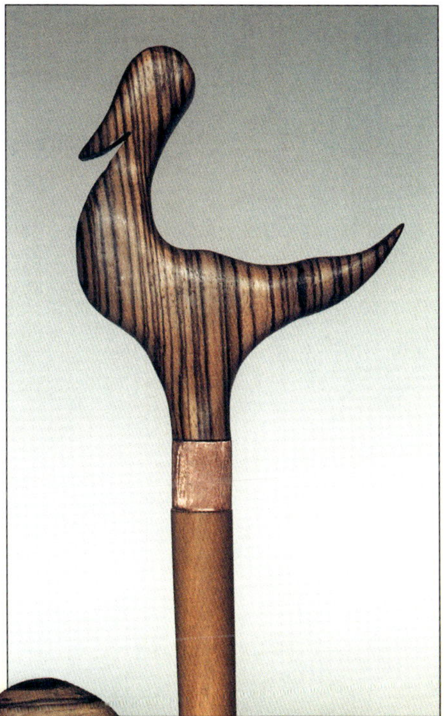

Abstract of a bird with vertical grain, five by five inches, with a brass corrugated collar.

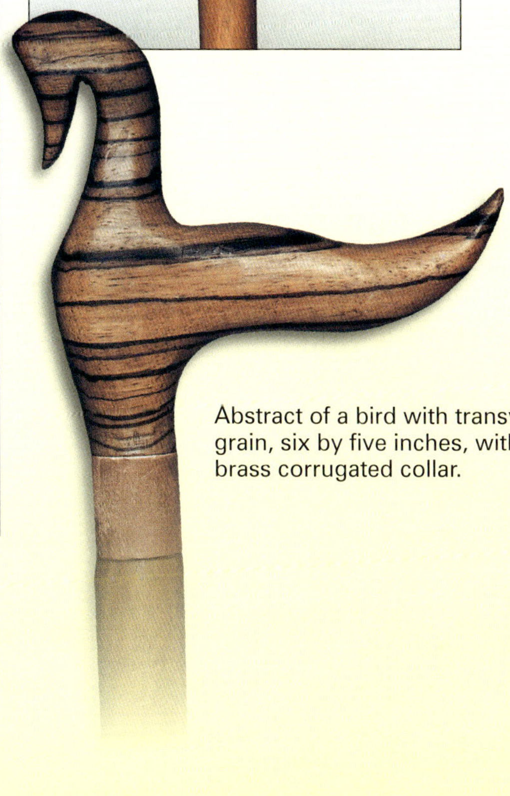

Abstract of a bird with transverse grain, six by five inches, with a brass corrugated collar.

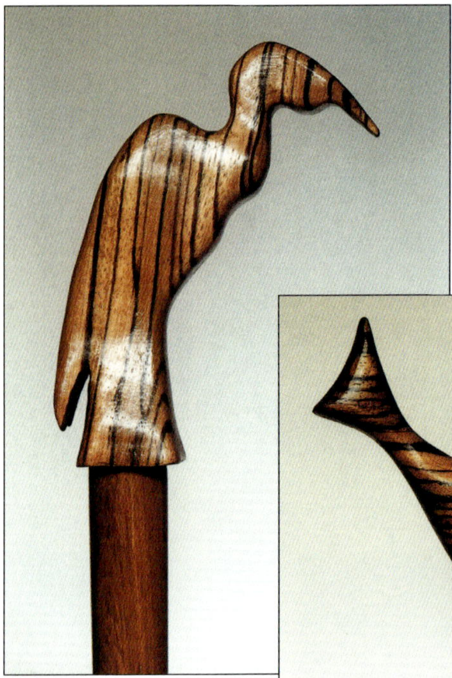

Abstract of a bird with vertical grain, four by five and a half inches with no connecting ring.

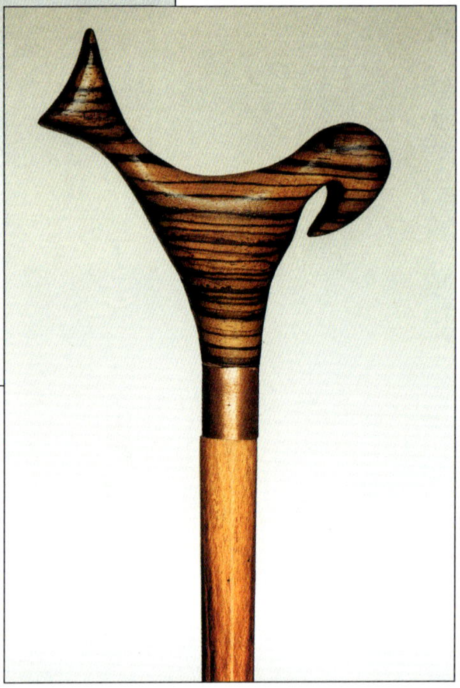

Abstract of a bird with transversely placed grain and corrugated collar, five by five inches.

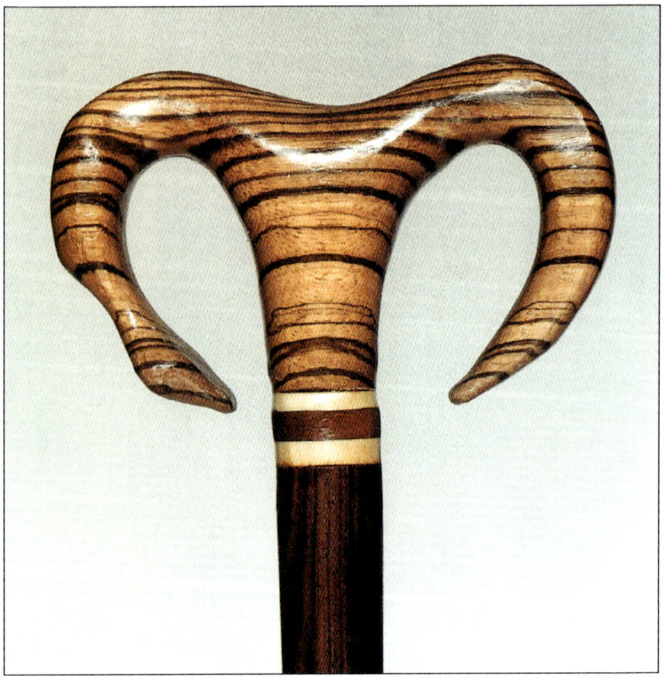

Abstract of a bird with horizontal grain, three by five inches. The connecting ring is in holly wood.

Abstract of a bird combining three varieties of wood, zebra, ebony, and zircote, five by six inches, with a brass corrugated collar.

Handles in Lower Relief

Large Tau handle with carvings of elongated mythological faces. The shaft is in rosewood. It is 7 1/2 x 9 inches with a connecting ring of buffalo horn.

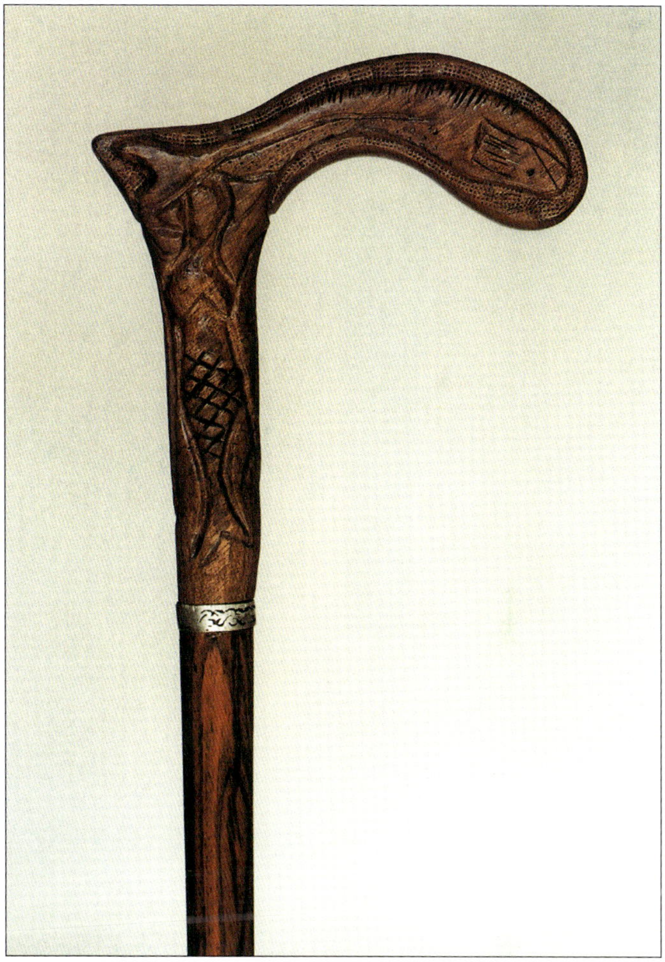

Tau handle, 7 x 7 inches, with carvings of sea animals: a sea horse is on one side and a mermaid on the opposite side, with a silver connecting ring. The shaft is in rosewood.

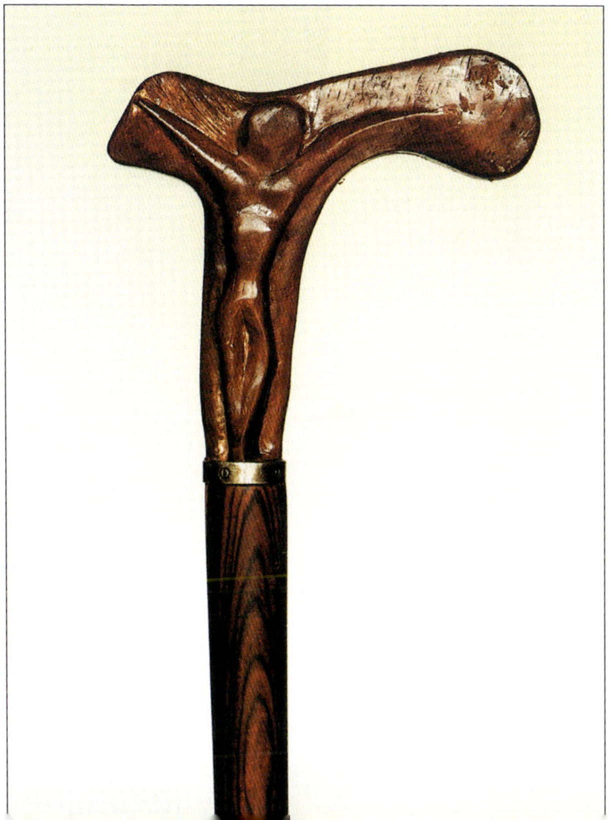

Tau handle in low relief of a woman. One side is the front of the body; the opposite side is a lateral view of the body, 5 x 5 inches, with a silver collar and a cocobola shaft.

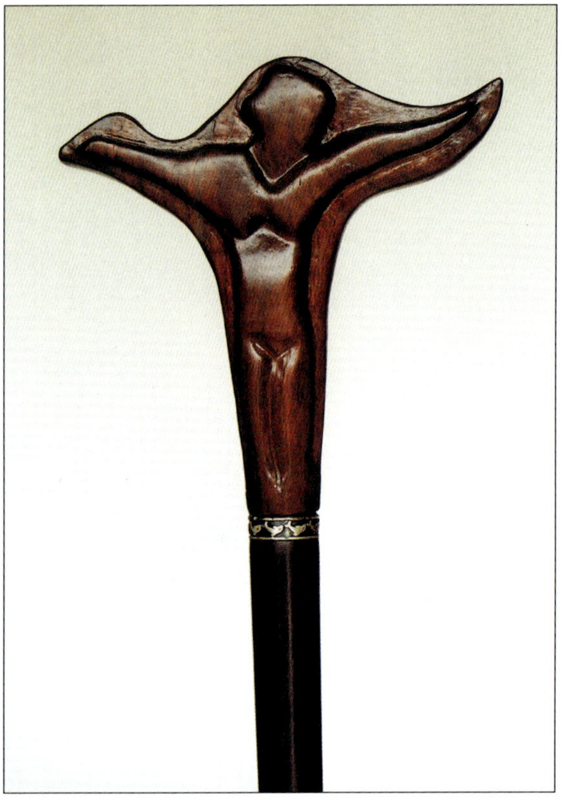

T-shaped handle in low relief of a nude woman. One side is the front; the opposite side is the back; 6 1/2 x 6 1/2 inches with a rosewood shaft.

T-shaped handles with carvings of birds in both faces, 5 x 6 1/2 inches, with a silver collar and a rosewood shaft.

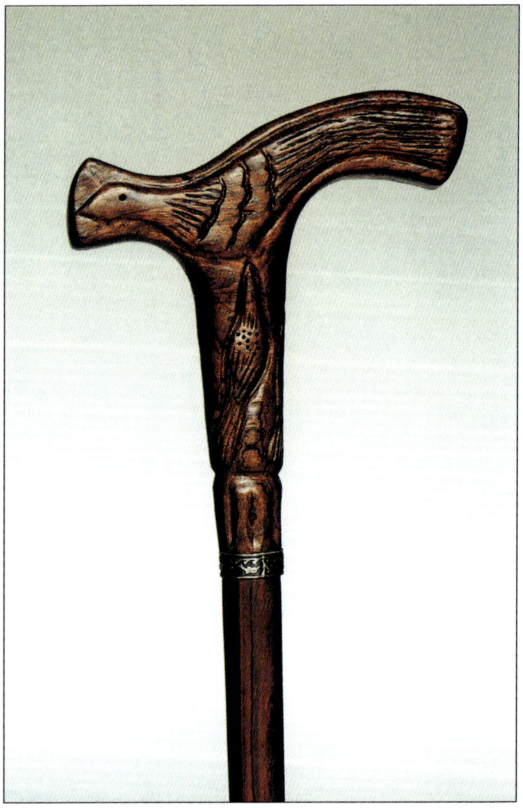

Tau-shaped handle of birds on both faces, with a silver collar, rosewood shaft, six by six inches handle.

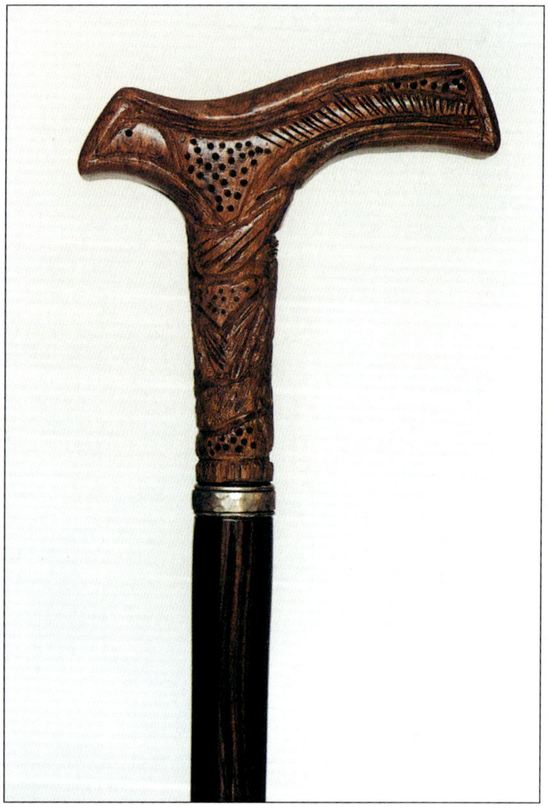

Tau-shaped handle with carvings of birds, 5 x 5 inches, and a silver collar with a cocobola shaft.

Five Canes With Lip-type Handles of Birds in Colorplay and Different Varieties of Wood

Twisted Lip-type handle in ebony. The body of the bird is in holly and ebony wood. The head is in ebony. The 9 x 8 inches handle has a silver collar.

Lip/mouth type handle in zebrawood with an amber stone. The bird is in ebony Colorplay wood, the wings in Patriot Colorplay wood, and the head in holly ebony wood, 9 x 9 inches.

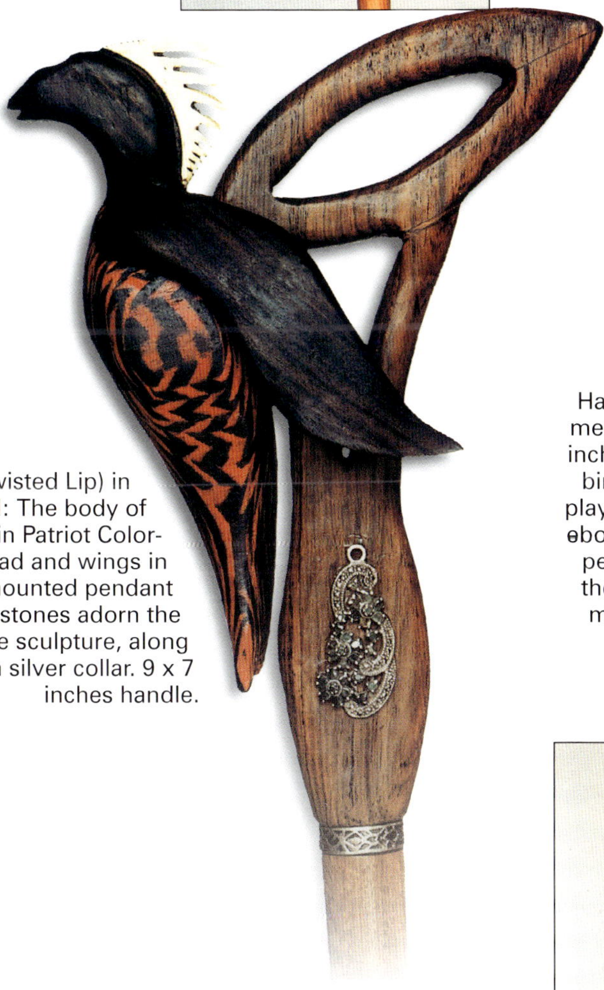

Type L (Twisted Lip) in Mora wood: The body of the bird is in Patriot Colorplay, the head and wings in ebony. A mounted pendant with gemstones adorn the base of the sculpture, along with a silver collar. 9 x 7 inches handle.

Handle in ebony wood measuring 7 1/2 x 5 1/2 inches. The body of the bird is in Patriot Colorplay wood, the wings in ebony. A mounted ruby pendant is attached to the bird. The handle is mounted with a silver connecting ring.

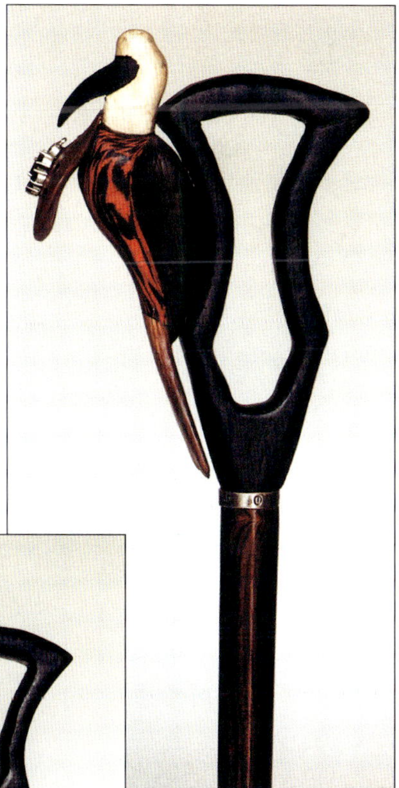

The Handle is in ebony wood, measures 8 x 8 inches, and has a connecting silver ring. The body of the bird is in Santa Fe Colorplay wood. The wings are of Eclipse Colorplay wood. A mounted square gemstone is attached to the handle.

Handles in Holly Wood

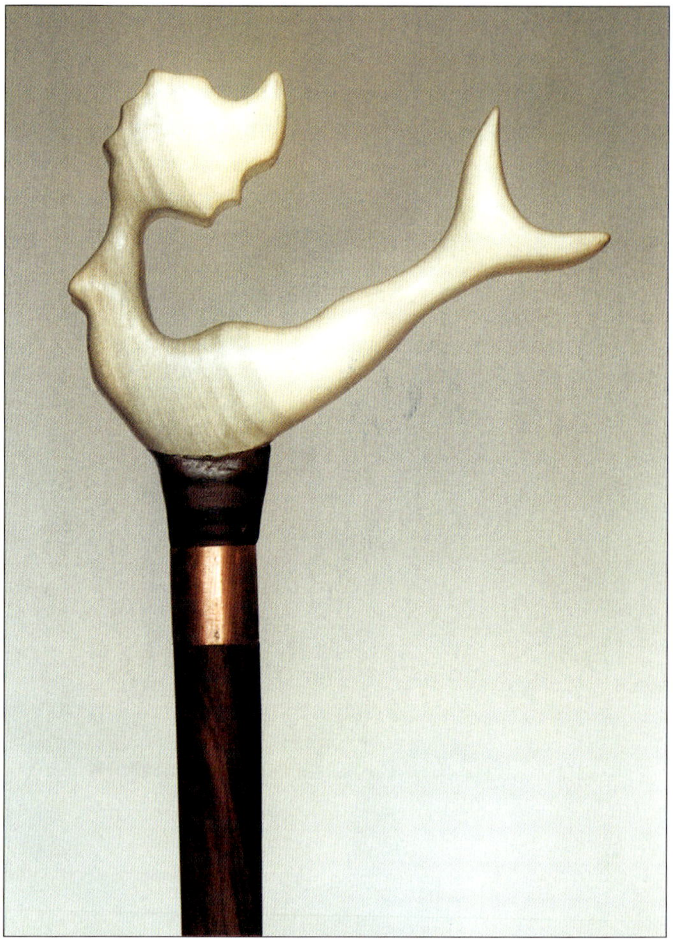

A mermaid with a backward twisted body. Corrugated brass collar. 4 1/2 x 6 inches handle.

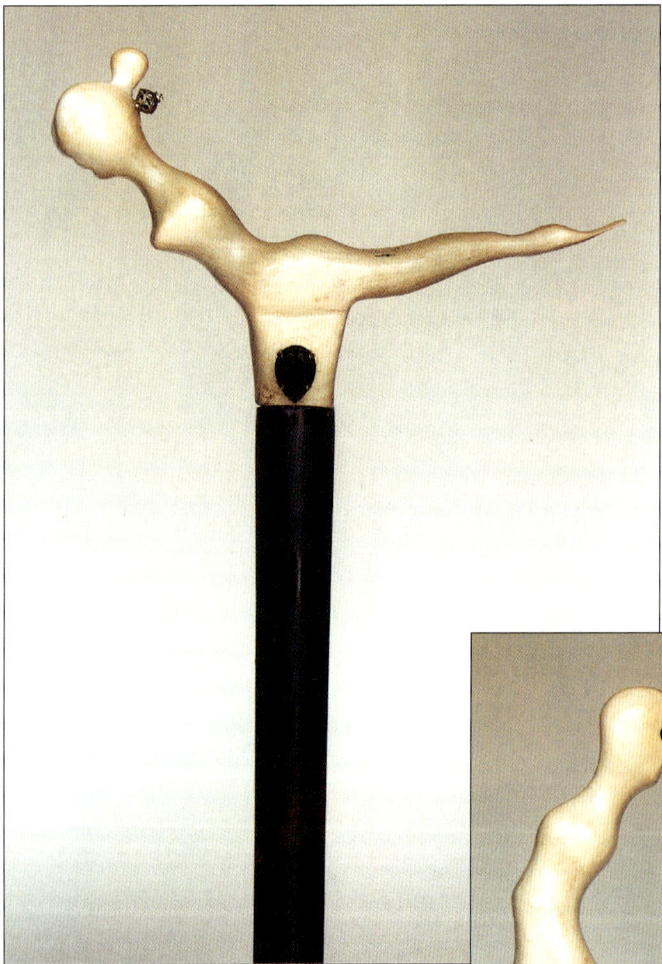

Body of a woman with a black stone and no connecting ring, 7 1/4 x 4 1/2 inches handle.

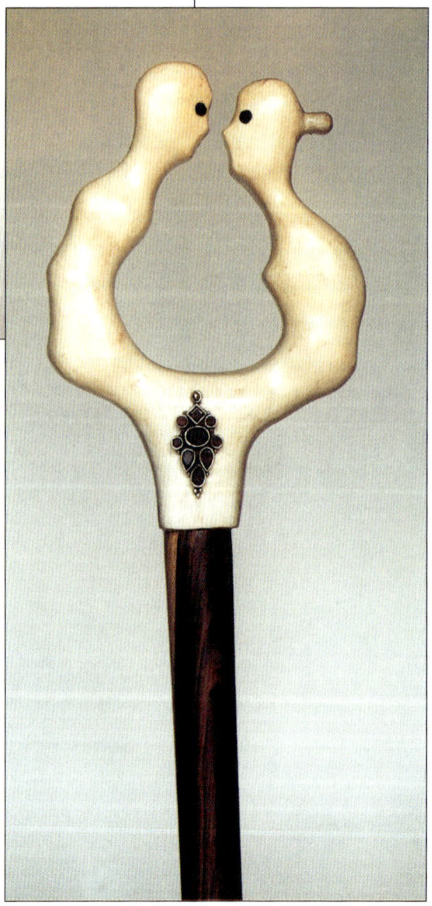

A couple, a man and a woman, facing each other with a mounted Black Onyx pendant adorning the sculpture. There is no connecting ring. 4 1/2 x 7 inches handle.

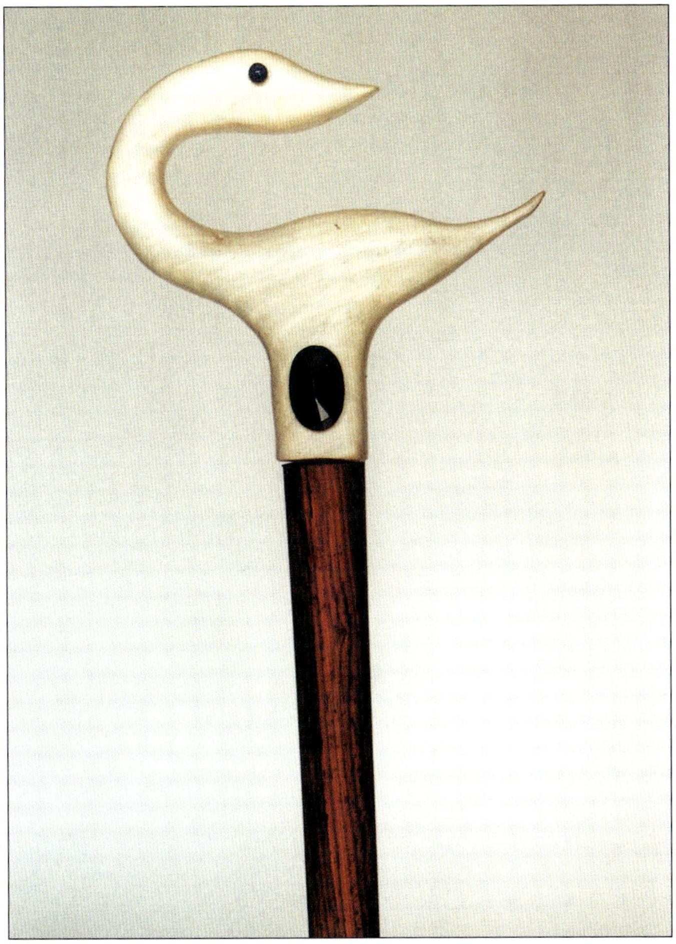

Abstract of a bird with a large unframed onyx stone, no connecting ring, 5 x 5 inches.

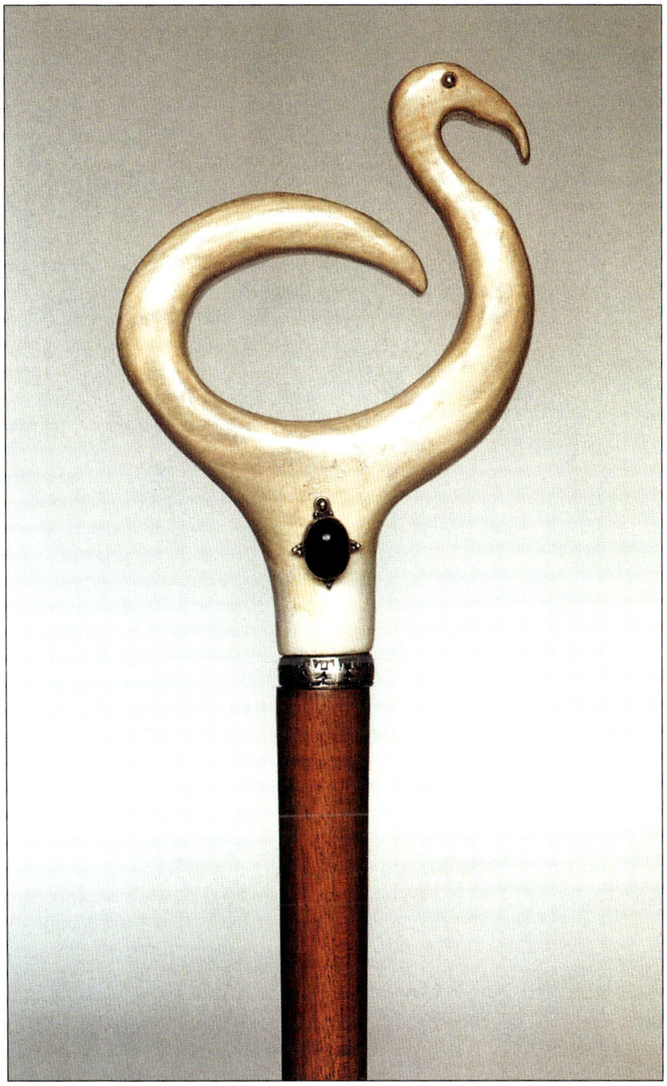

Sculpture of a bird in circular fashion adorned with a framed black stone and a silver connecting ring. 6 1/2 by 5 inches handle.

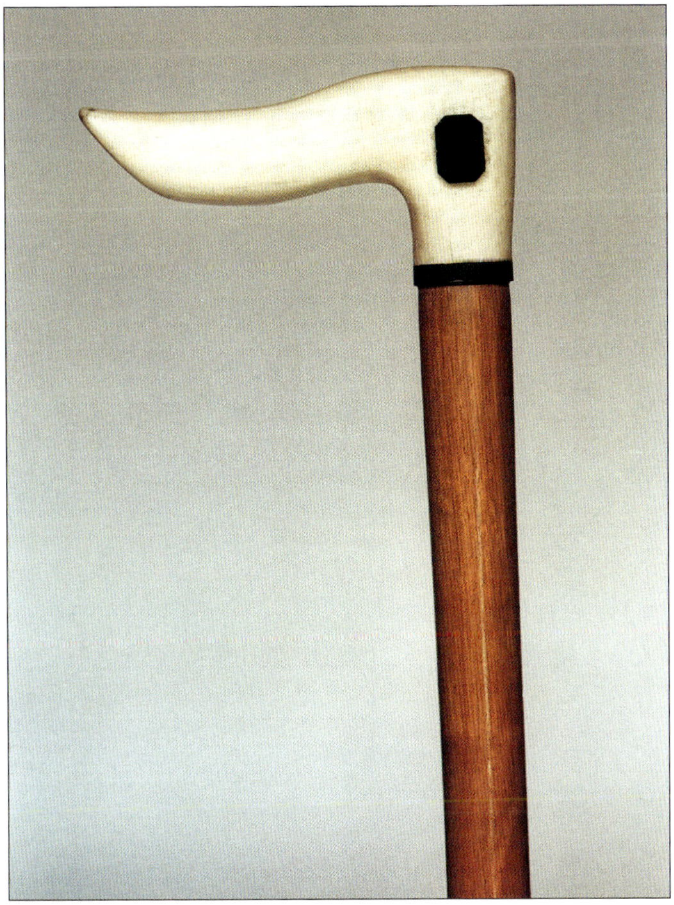

L-shaped handle with green and black gemstones. There is no collar. 4 x 5 inches handle.

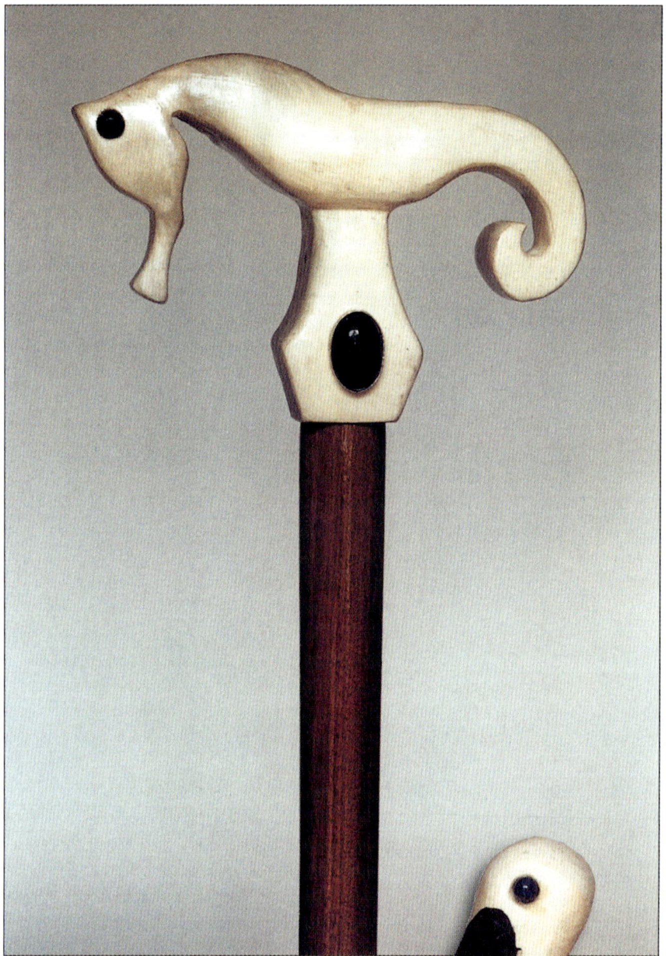

A seahorse in holly wood with a mounted black stone, 6 x 4 1/2 inches.

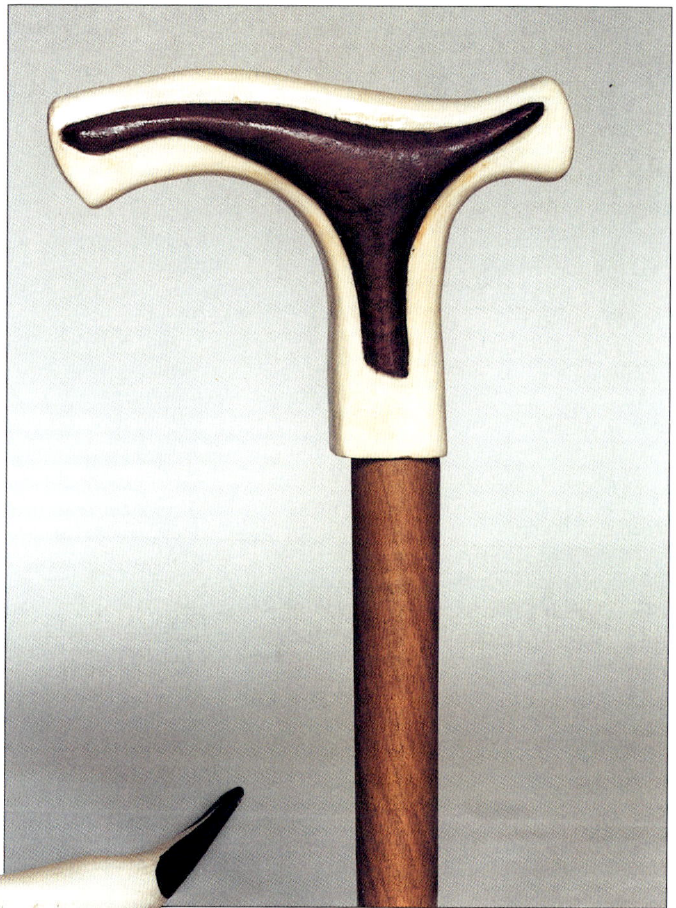

A Tau handle of holly wood with a superimposed abstract of a bird. The handle measures 4 x 6 inches and has no connecting ring.

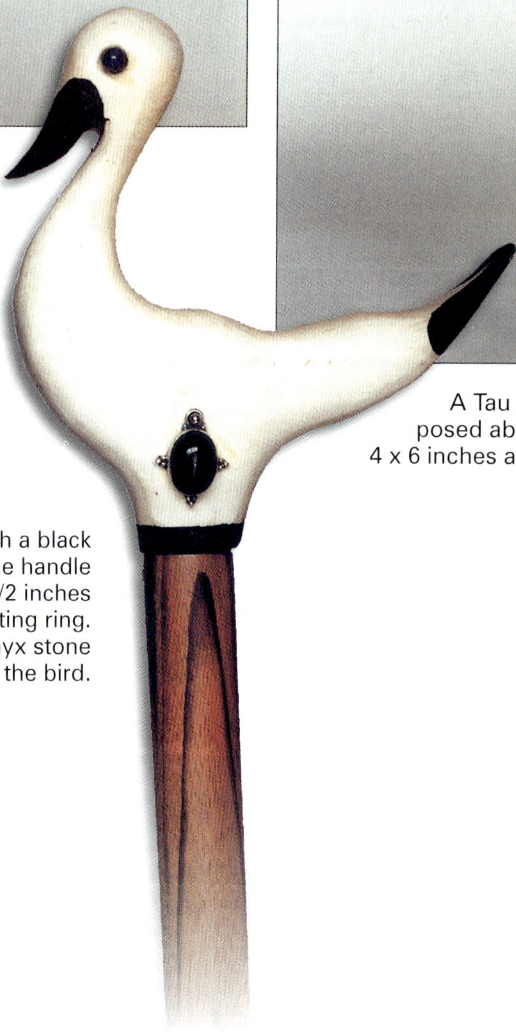

A bird in holly wood with a black painted beak and tail. The handle measures 5 1/2 x 5 1/2 inches and has a wood connecting ring. A mounted black onyx stone adorns the bird.

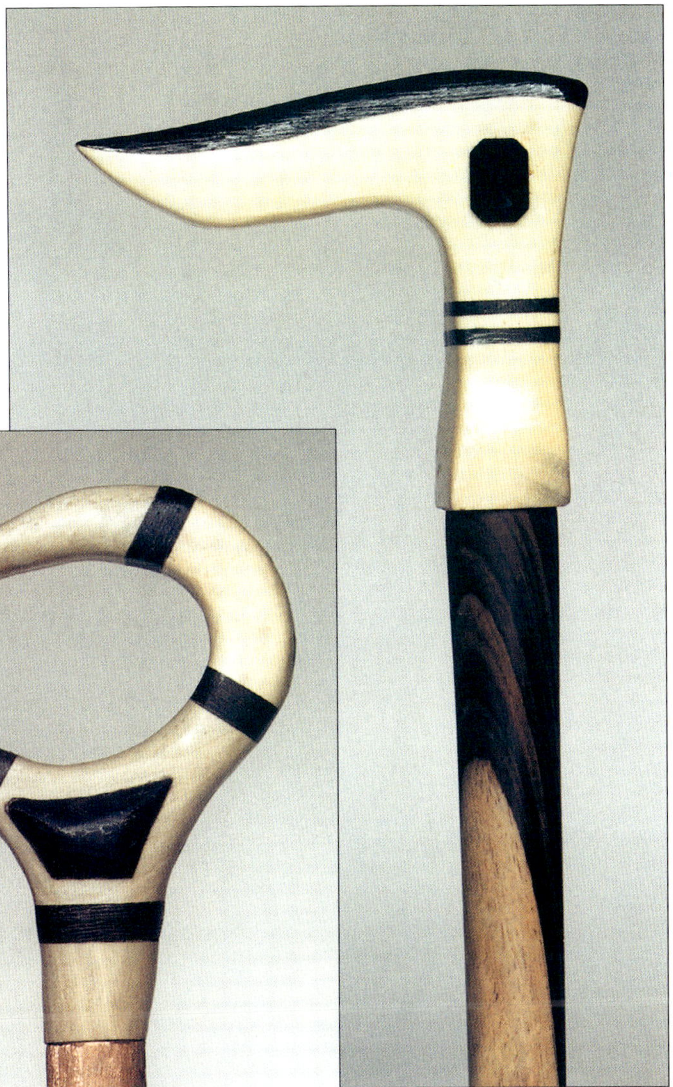

L-shaped handle with ebony decorations and a black stone. The handle measures 3 1/2 x 4 1/2 inches and has no connecting ring.

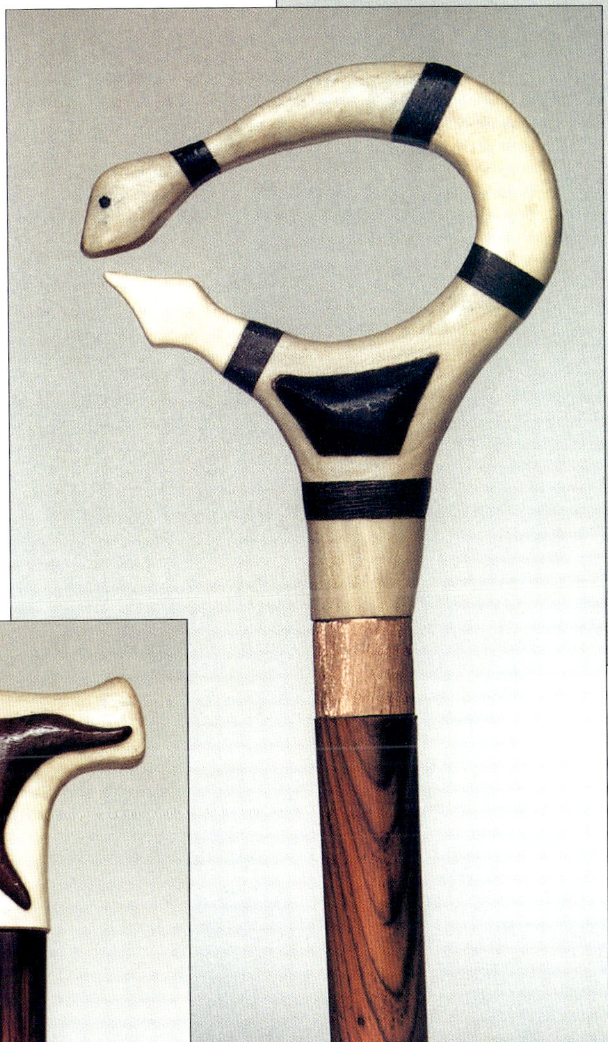

Circular shaped handle in holly wood of a snake decorated with ebony wood. The handle measures 5 1/2 x 4 1/2 inches and has a corrugated brass colored collar.

Tau-shaped handle in holly wood with a superimposed abstract of a bird. The handle measures 4 x 4 inches and has no connecting ring.

L-shaped handle in holly wood with the superimposed body of a woman in ebony. The handle measures 3 1/2 x 4 1/2 inches.

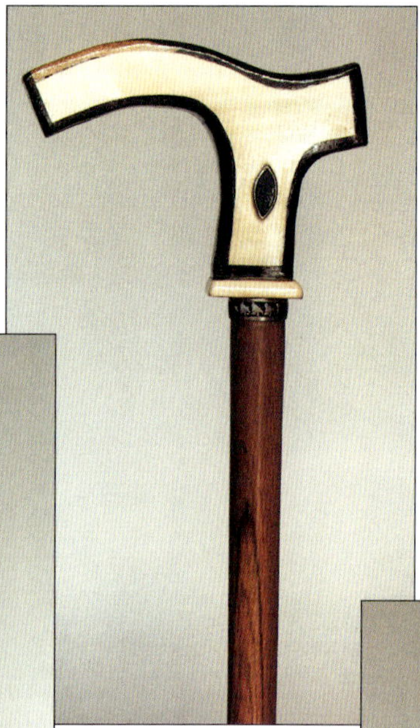

Crook-shaped handle in holly wood framed with Macassar ebony and ornamented with a black stone. The handle measures 3 x 5 inches and has a silver collar.

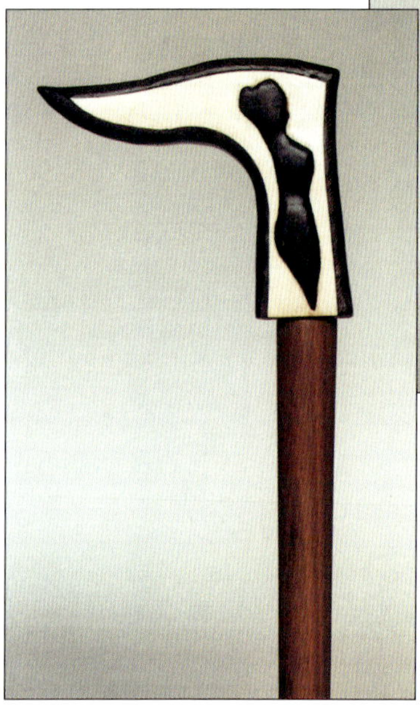

L-shaped handle framed with Macassar ebony and adorned with a superimposed body of a woman. The handle measures 4 x 5 inches and has no collar.

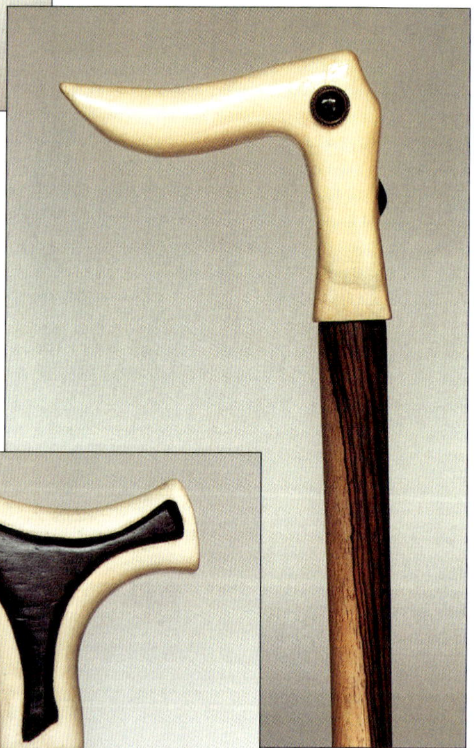

L-shaped handle with a large rectangular, black onyx stone without a mount. The handle measures 2 x 4 1/2 inches and has a black wood collar.

Crook type handle in holly wood with a superimposed abstract of a bird. The handle measures 6 x 4 inches and has a silver collar.

Lip-type Handles

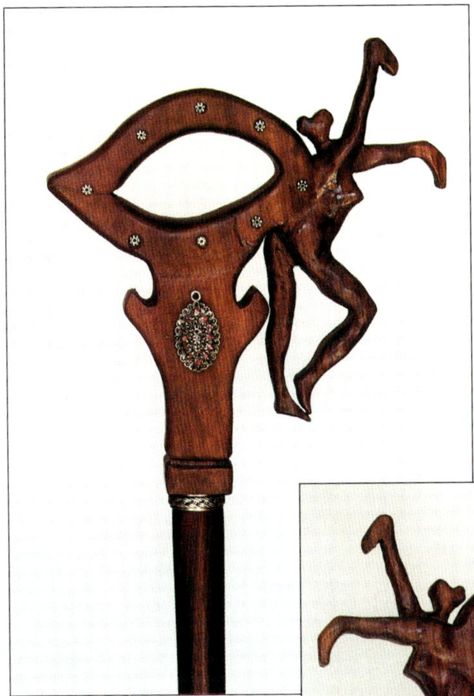

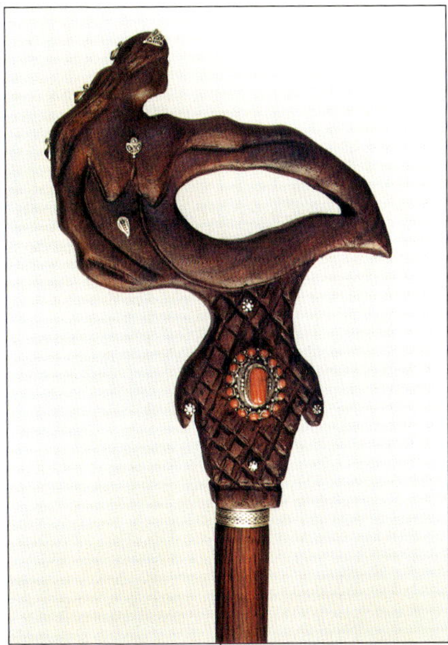

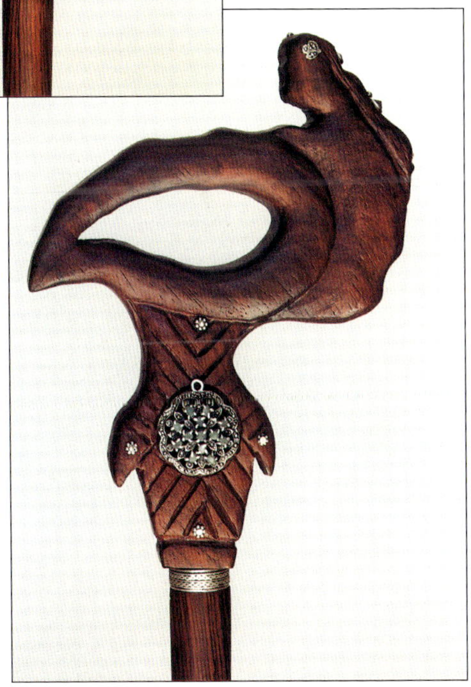

Lip-type handle in Mara wood with the body of a woman on one side. The two sides of the handle are adorned with two different gemstone pendants. The body is adorned with small silver studs with and handle is finished with a silver collar. The handle measures 8 1/2 x 5 inches. It is a one piece, three-dimensional sculpture.

Lip-type handle with a female figure on one side. The figure is a three-dimensional carving. The handle is adorned with two different gemstone pendants and small silver studs. The handle measures 8 /1/4 x six inches and has a double silver collar.

Lip-type handle in Macassar ebony with attached nude of a woman. The woman is a three-dimensional sculpture. It was carved separately and attached to the shaft. Two different pendants adorn the two faces of the handle. A gemstone and a pearl adorn the head. The handle measures 9 x 5 inches and has a silver collar.

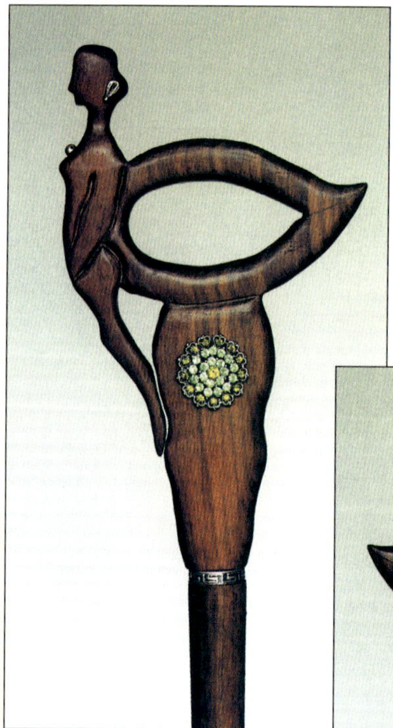

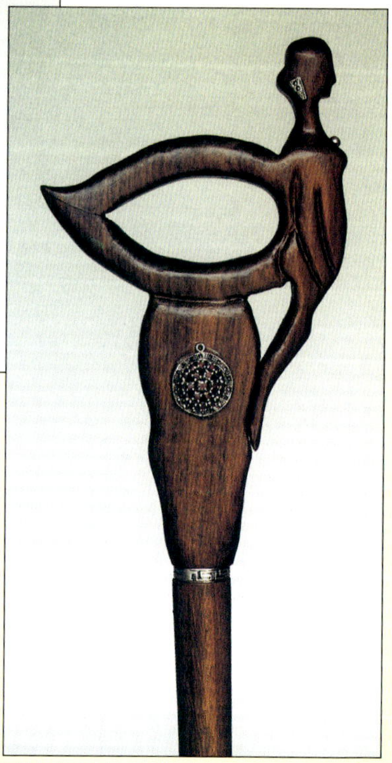

Lip-type handle in Mara wood with attached female body is sculpted in one piece in three dimensions. Each side of the handle has a different gemstone pendant and several small silver studs. The handle measures 8 x 7 inches and has a double silver collar.

Lip-type handle in Macassar ebony with attached abstract of a bird. One-piece sculpture. A pendant adorns the bottom of the sculptured handle. The handle measures 7 1/4 x 4 1/2 inches and has a silver collar.

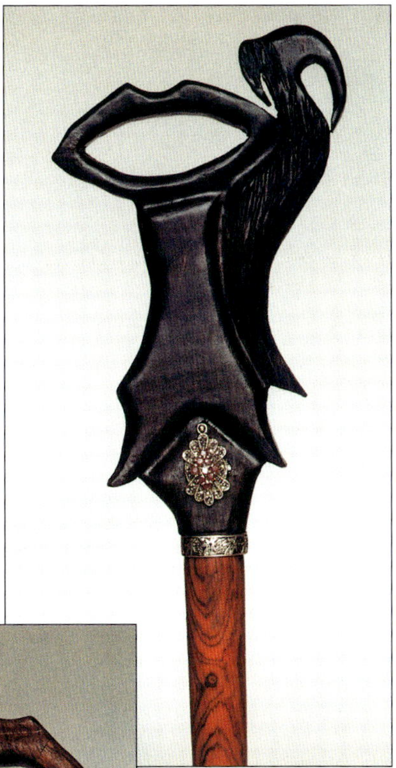

Lip-type handle in Macassar ebony with a male dancer attached on one side. This is a one-piece sculpture with the handle. The dancer is a three-dimensional carving. The handle measures 7 x 7 inches and has a double silver ring.

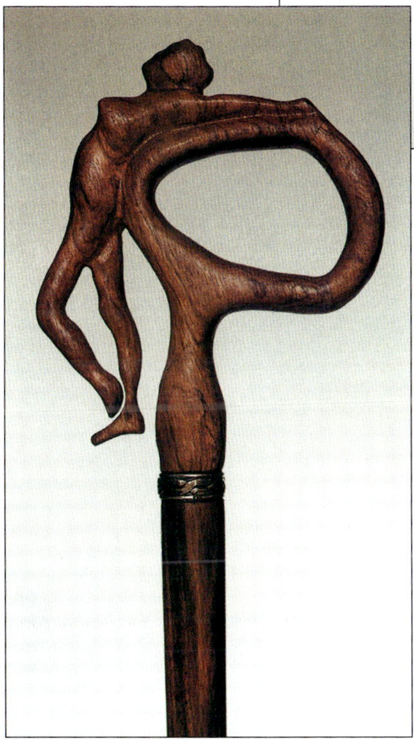

Lip-type Honduras rosewood handle with an attached nude female body; the handle is a one-piece sculpture with the body, which is a three-dimensional sculpture. The handle measures 6 3/4 x 5 1/2 inches and has a double silver collar.

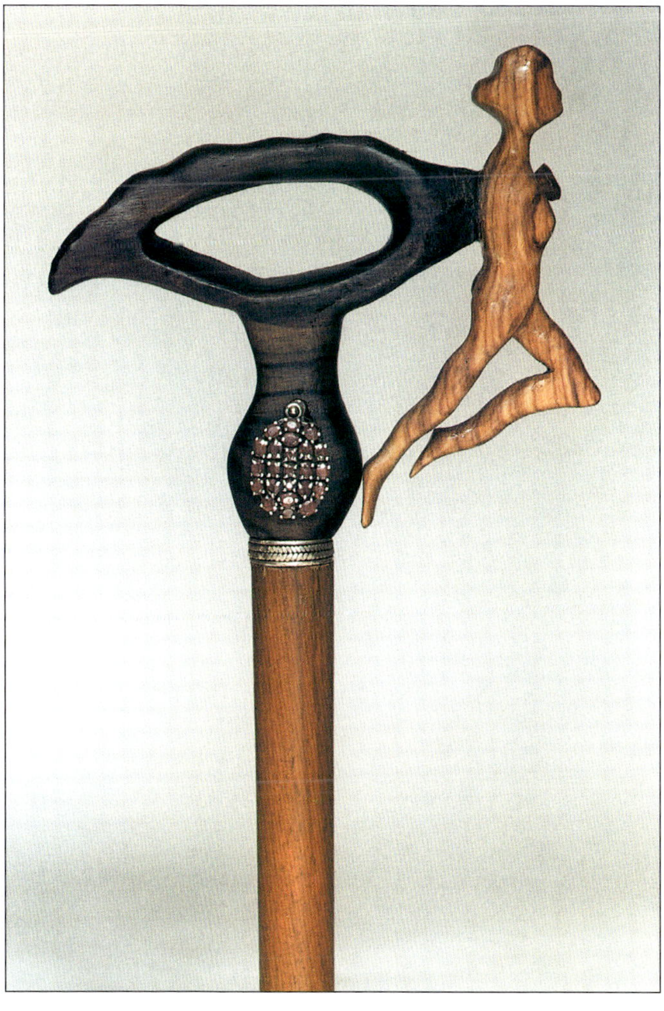

Lip-type handle in Macassar ebony with an attached female body in tulipwood. The female body is a three-dimensional sculpture carved separately from the handle. A ruby stone is attached to the breast and a ruby pendant is attached to the handle. The handle measures 6 1/2 x 6 1/2 inches and has a silver collar.

A twisted lip-type handle in Macassar ebony with a nude of a woman in lateral view. A mounted gemstone pendant adorns the base of the handle. The handle measures 5 1/2 x 5 1/2 inches and has a silver collar.

A mouth-type handle, the upper lip is a fish sculptured in Macassar ebony. A pearl and a mounted amber stone adorn the base of the sculpture. The handle measures 4 x 5 inches and has a silver connecting ring.

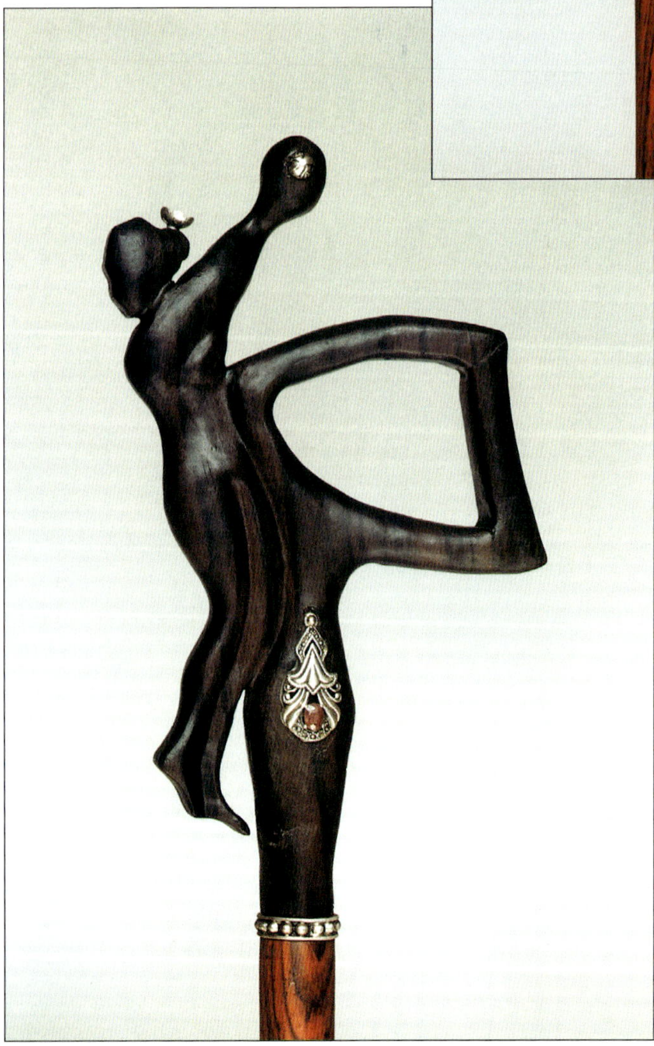

A mouth-type handle in Macassar ebony with a woman holding a ball. Small silver studs and a silver pendant with a ruby adorn the sculpture. The handle measures 9 x 5 inches and has a silver collar.

The wing of a butterfly is the place to grasp the handle. A mounted gem pendant adorns the base of the sculpture. The handle measures 6 x 4 inches and has a silver collar.

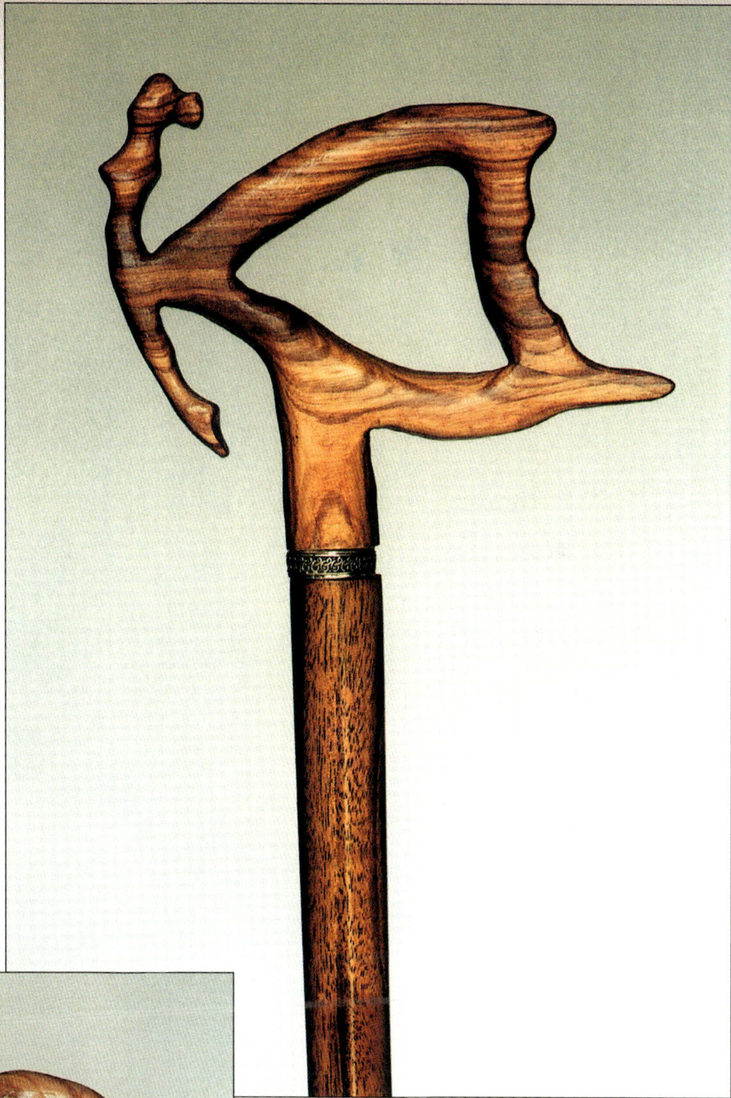

A female body attached to a heart-shaped handle in tulipwood. The handle measures 6 x 5 1/4 inches and has a silver collar.

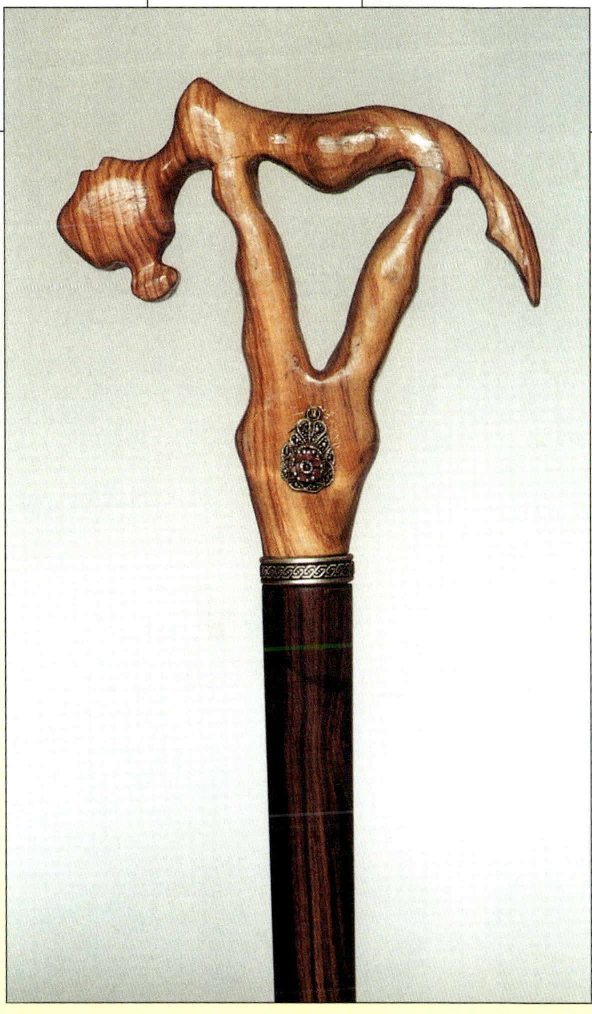

A female body in tulipwood suspended by two extended arms. A mounted pendant is at the base of the sculpture. The handle measures 5 1/2 x 5 1/2 inches and has a silver collar.

A female body attached to a heart-shaped handle in Honduras rosewood. The handle measures 6 1/4 x 4 1/2 inches and has no connecting ring.

A butterfly wing is the place to grasp the Honduras rosewood handle. A framed amber stone adorns the base of the sculpture. The handle measures 6 1/4 x 4 1/2 inches and has a silver collar.

Double-deck Handles with Mini-sculptures

A round handle in Honduras rosewood with a miniature sculpture of a bird at the center. The bird has been carved separately and inserted into the handle with glue and a wooden rod. A black mounted stone adorns the base. The handle measures 8 x 5 inches and has a silver connecting ring.

A lip-style handle in Honduras rosewood with an abstract miniature sculpture of a bird inserted at the base of the handle. Two black mounted hard stones adorn the handle. The handle measures 9 x 5 inches and has a silver connecting ring.

A lip-style handle in Honduras rosewood with a miniature sculptured bird at the center. The handle measures 9 x 5 inches and has a silver connecting ring.

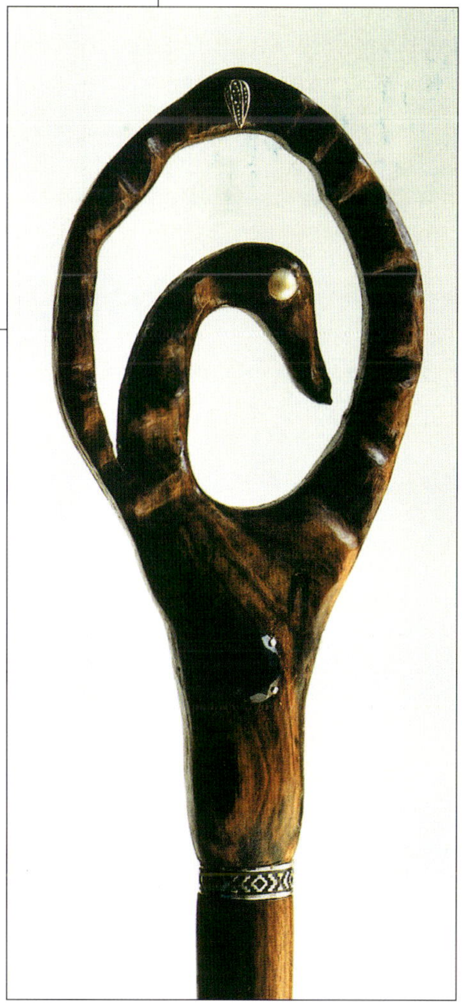

The round handle in Costa Rica rosewood has a bird at the center (one-piece) and a black stone and pearl adorning the handle. The handle measures 8 x 3 1/2 inches and has a silver connecting ring.

Double-deck handle in Marcasite ebony with a white bone cross in the lower deck. The handle measures 10 x 5 inches and has a double silver connecting ring. Overall cane length is 37 inches.

Double-deck handles in zebrawood with a miniature sculpture of a woman in white bone. The handle measures 12 x 5 inches and has a double silver connecting ring. Overall cane length is 36 inches.

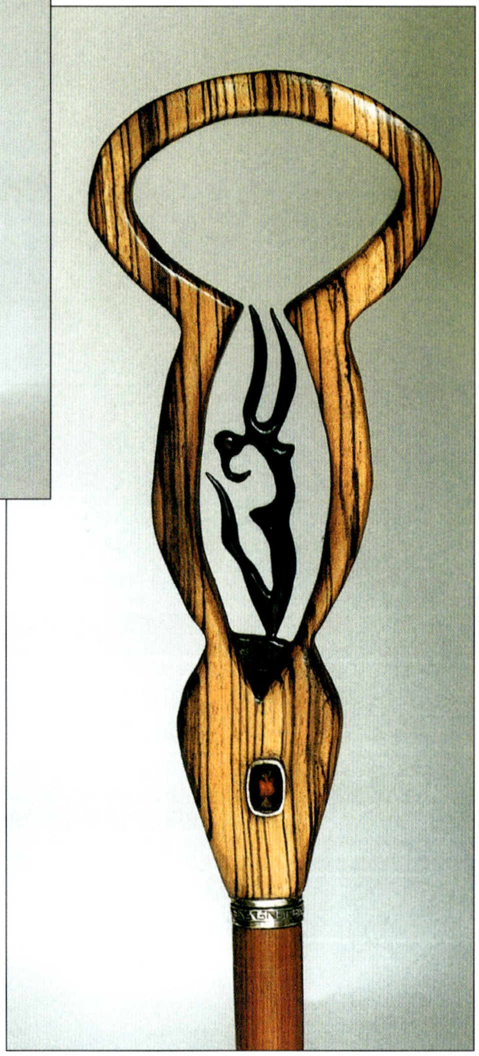

Double-deck handle in zebrawood with a woman in rosewood in the lower deck. A mounted stone adorns the base. The handle measures 9 x 5 inches and has a double silver connecting ring. Overall cane length is 37 inches.

Elaborate Sculptured Handles

This handle of Honduran rosewood features a man and woman facing each other. The figures are connected at the base of the handle. The handle measures 8 x 4 1/2 inches and has a one-piece connecting ring in holly wood.

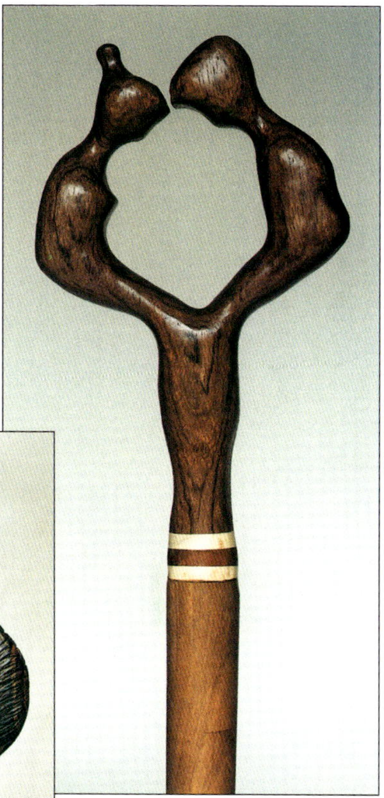

Two different birds were used as handles of a vase carved from cocobola. The handle measures 5 x 5 inches and has no connecting ring.

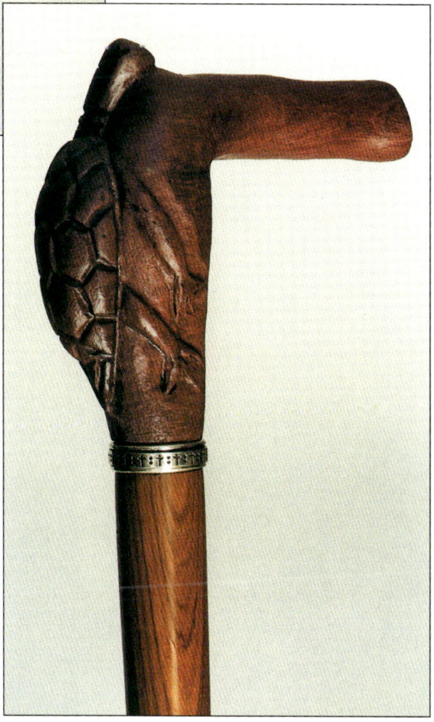

L-shaped handle in purple heart wood with a carved turtle. The handle measures 4 x 4 inches and has a silver connecting ring.

An elaborate sculpture in wenge wood representing a dancing couple, a man and a woman. Four mounted brown stones adorn the four faces of the handle's base. The three pieces comprising the handle are connected with wooden rods. The handle measures 10 x 4 1/2 inches and has a silver connecting ring.

Handles with Female Bodies

A large, elaborate sculpture in cocobola, 12 x 5 inches, representing a woman riding on top of an African ostrich. Several pearls and a custom-made pendant with rubies adorn one face of the sculpture. The shaft is rosewood and has a silver collar. Overall cane length is 40 inches.

Large three-dimensional sculpture, 9 x 5 inches, in redwood, featuring a woman riding a mythological animal. Both faces are adorned with custom-made pendants with gemstones and pearls. The shaft is in cocobola wood and has a silver collar. Overall cane length is 40 inches.

A nude woman on top of an amphora, which is worked in low relief with birds in Honduras rosewood. The handle measures 6 1/2 x 4 1/2 and has a double silver collar. Overall cane length is 38 inches.

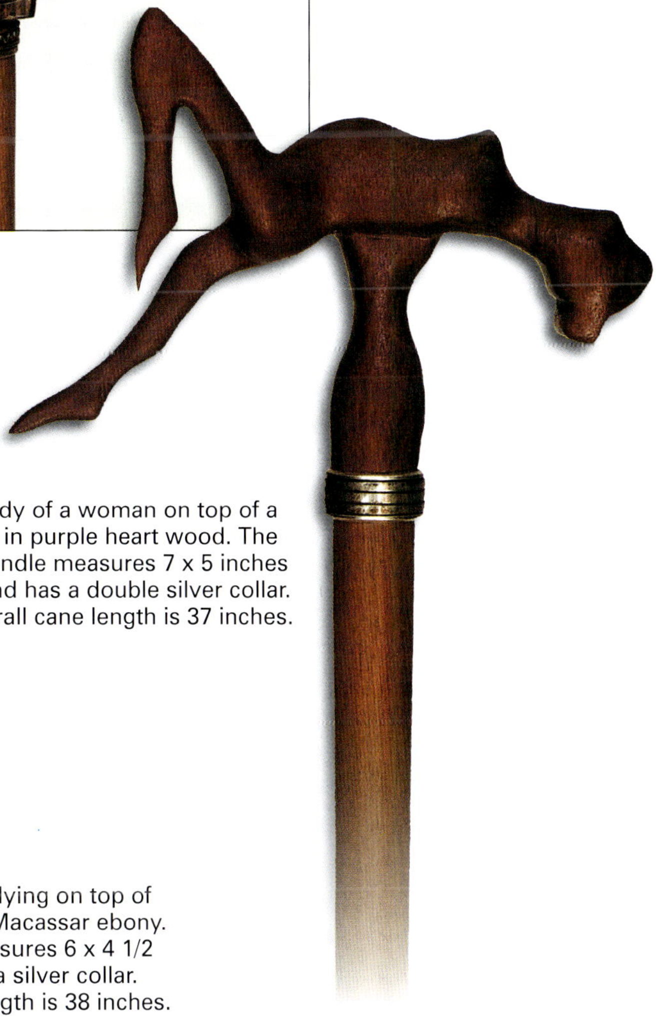

Body of a woman on top of a vase in purple heart wood. The handle measures 7 x 5 inches and has a double silver collar. Overall cane length is 37 inches.

A nude woman lying on top of an amphora in Macassar ebony. The handle measures 6 x 4 1/2 inches and has a silver collar. Overall cane length is 38 inches.

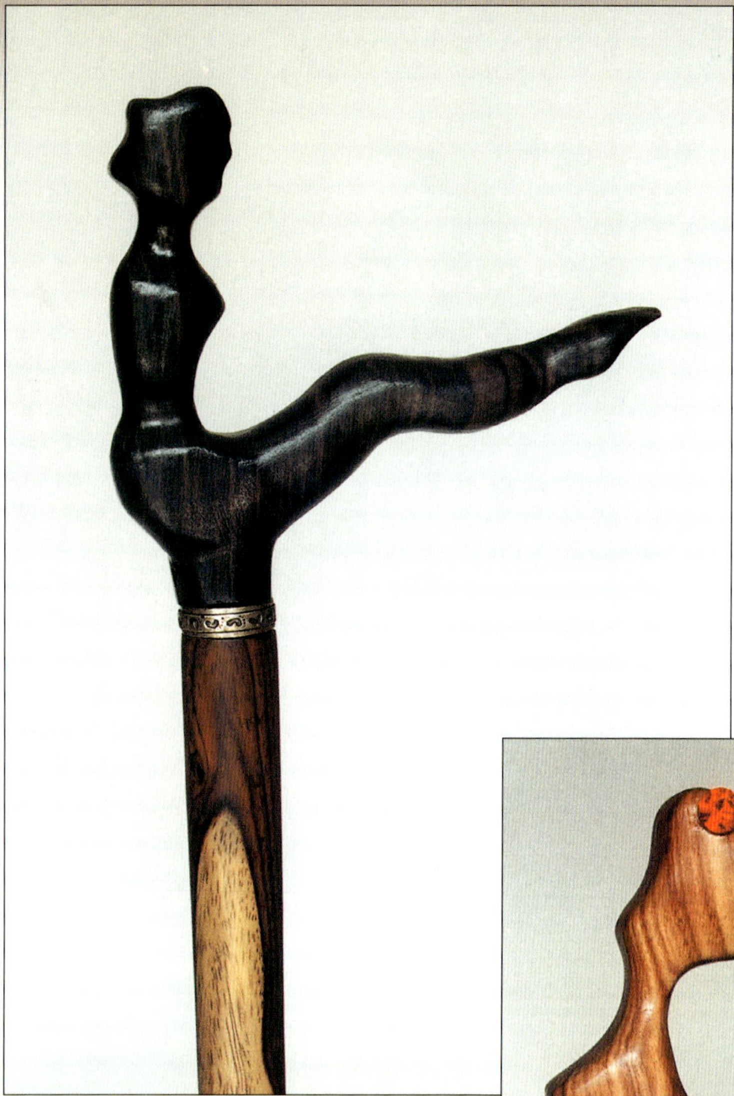

A nude woman sitting on top of an amphora in Macassar ebony. The handle measures 8 x 6 inches and has a double silver collar. Overall cane length is 36 inches.

A mermaid in tulipwood with a ruby at the base of the sculpture. The handle measures 6 x 4 inches and has a silver collar.

Woman with a comb and a framed amber stone at the base of the sculpture. The handle measures 8 x 4 inches and has a silver collar.

Sculpture similar to the previous example in Sicilian pear wood. The face and the braids are adorned with small stones and custom-made framed onyx pendant over the breast. The handle measures 6 x 4 inches and has a silver collar.

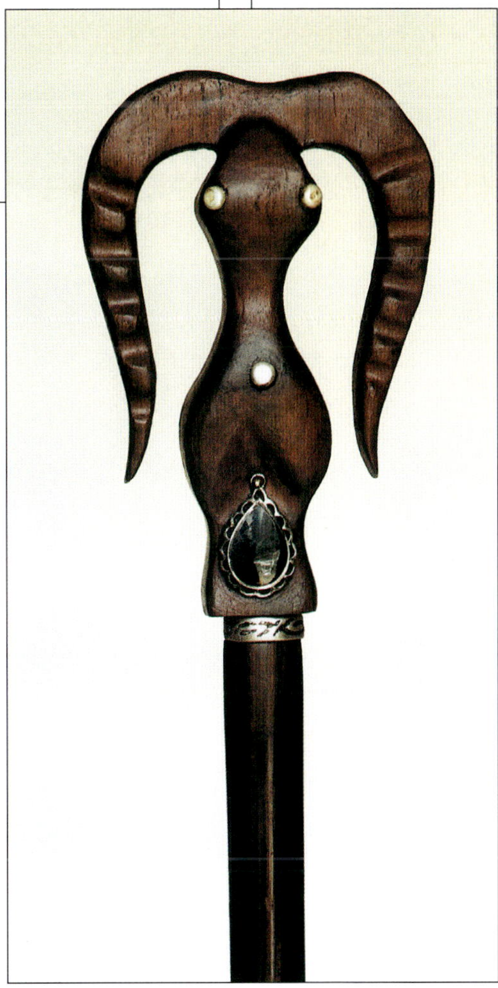

The bust of a woman with braids adorned with pearls and a framed black onyx stone at the base of the sculpture. The handle measures 6 1/2 x 4 1/2 inches and has a silver collar.

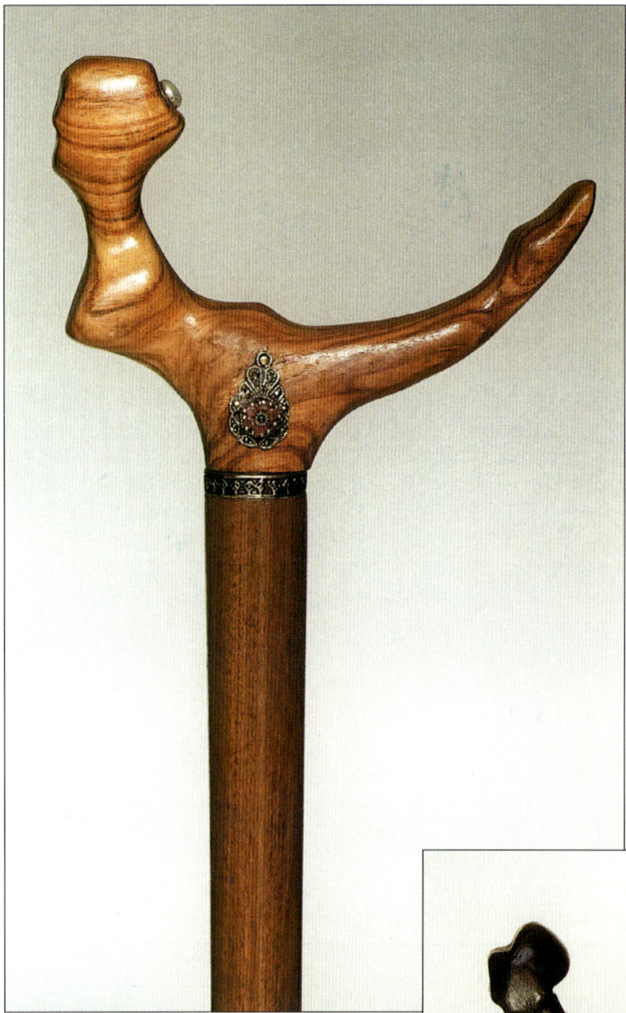

Nude of a woman in tulipwood adorned with a pearl and a pendant with small stones at the base of the sculpture. The handle measures 5 1/2 x 4 inches and has a silver collar.

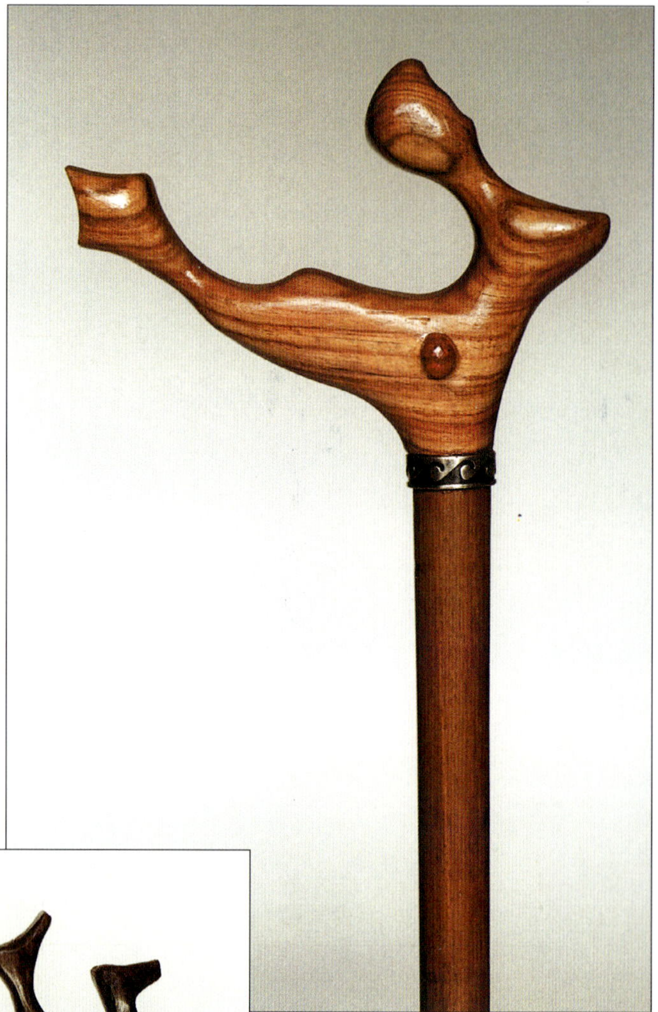

A mermaid in tulipwood adorned with a pendant with a ruby and a pearl. The handle measures 5 1/2 x 5 inches and has a silver collar.

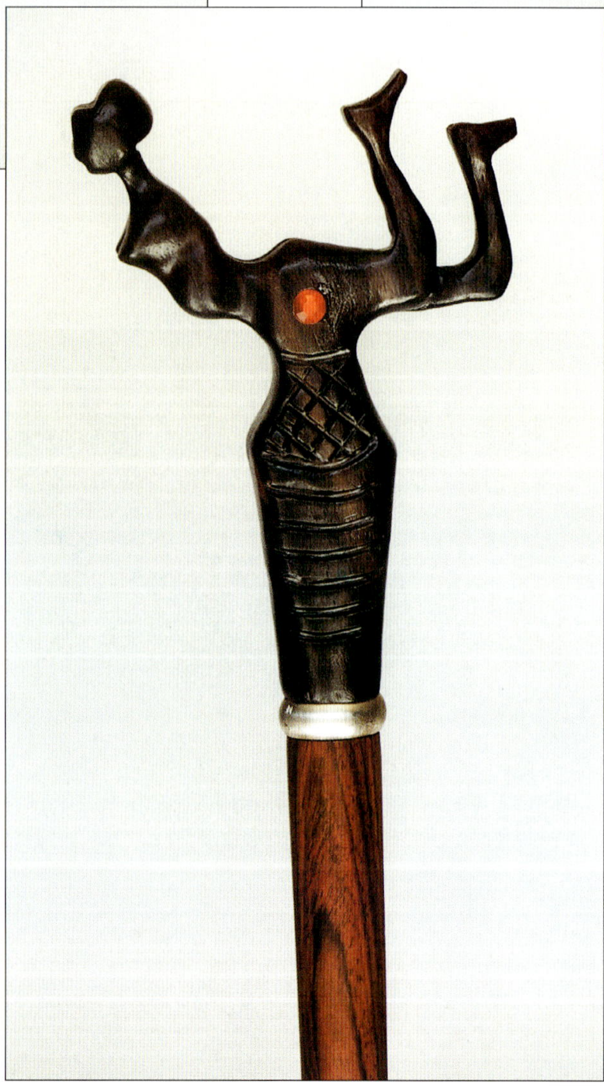

A woman in Macassar ebony adorned with a pearl and a ruby. The handle measures 5 x 5 inches and has a silver collar.

Triangular-shaped handle with the body of a woman in Macassar ebony. The handle measures 6 x 6 inches and has a silver collar.

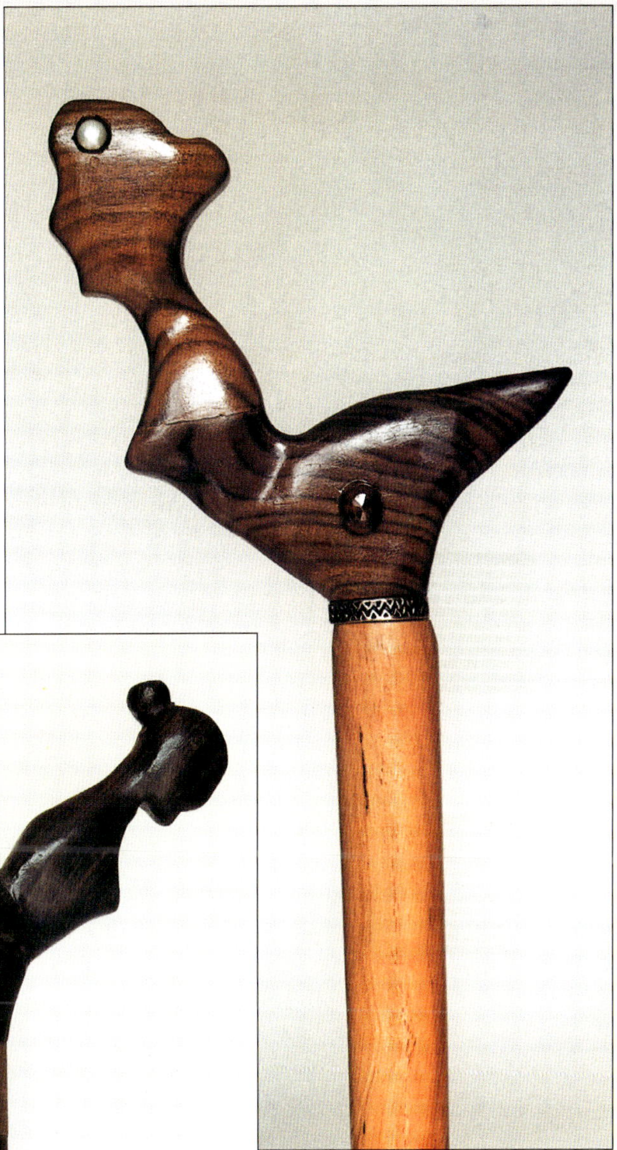

Nude of a woman in Macassar ebony. The handle measures 6 x 5 inches and has a double silver collar.

Nude of a woman in Macassar ebony with a long corrugated brass collar. The handle measurs 7 1/2 by 4 1/2 inches.

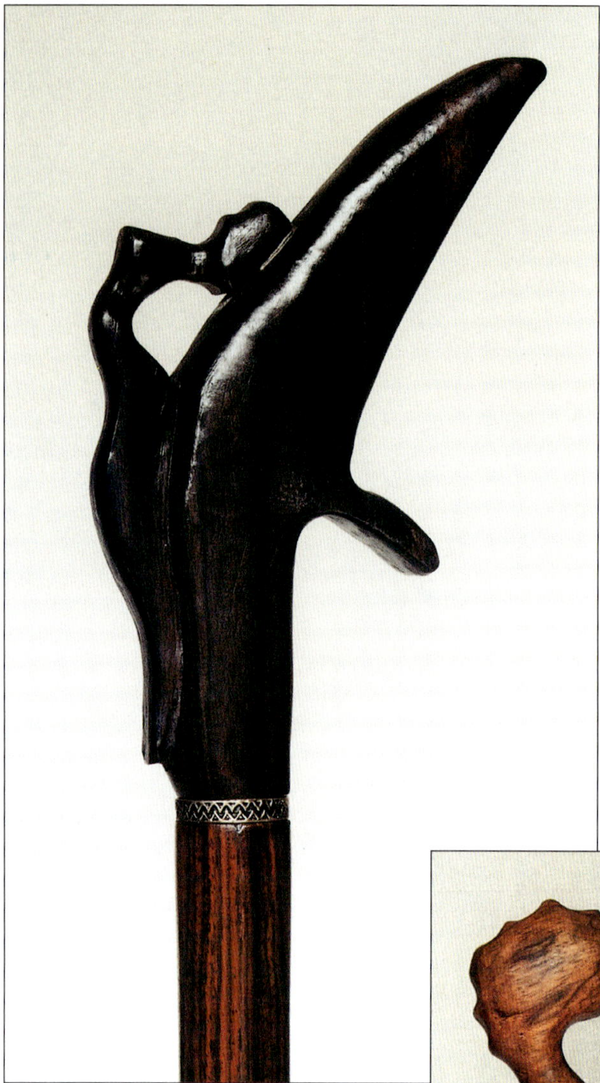

Nude of a woman in Macassar ebony lying on the wing of a butterfly. The handle measures 6 1/2 x 3 inches and has a silver collar.

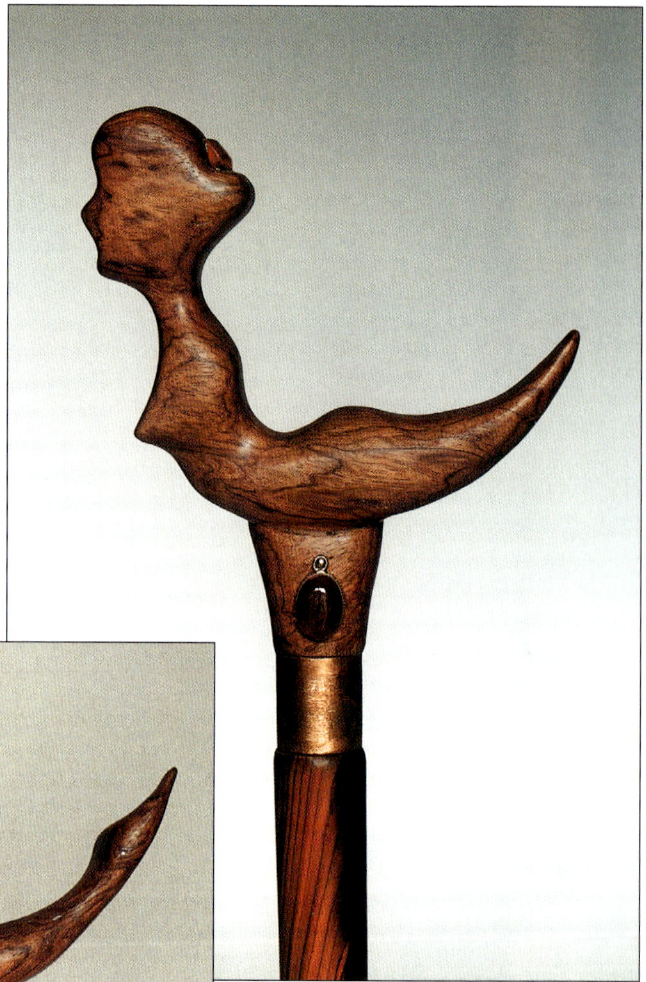

Body of a woman in Honduras rosewood adorned with a gemstone and an amber stone. The handle measures 5 x 6 inches and has a corrugated brass collar.

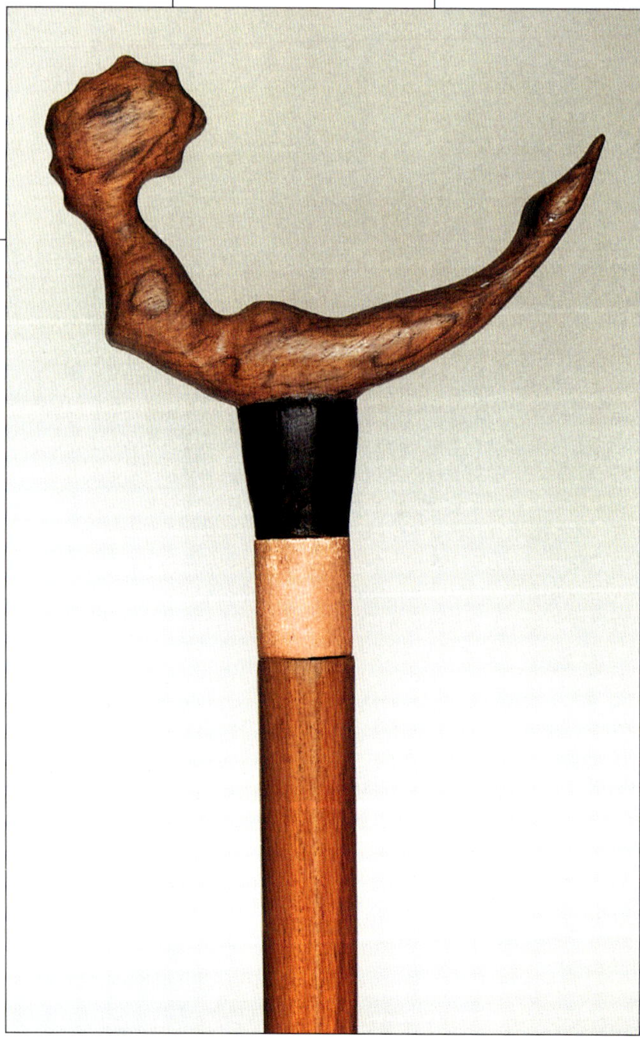

Body of a woman in rosewood and Macassar ebony. The handle measures 5 1/2 x 4 1/2 and has a corrugated brass collar.

A dancing couple connected by the neck adorn this two-piece handle, which measure 8 x 4 inches and has a silver connecting ring collar.

A female nude in hardwood adorned with a silver stud and a ruby pendant at the base. The handle measures 6 1/2 x 5 inches and has a silver collar.

Elaborate sculpture featuring four different birds connected through the head. The birds are carved from zebrawood. The upper part and the base of the handle are carved from Macassar ebony. Four different pendants decorate the base. The handle has a silver connecting ring.

Handles of Animals

A horse in cocobola wood on top of a vase. A square piece of holly wood was used as a connecting piece with the shaft. The handle measures 10 1/2 x 5 inches.

Another horse in Macassar ebony on top of an amphora. The handle measures 8 1/2 x 5 inches. A square of holly wood is substituted for the usual connecting ring.

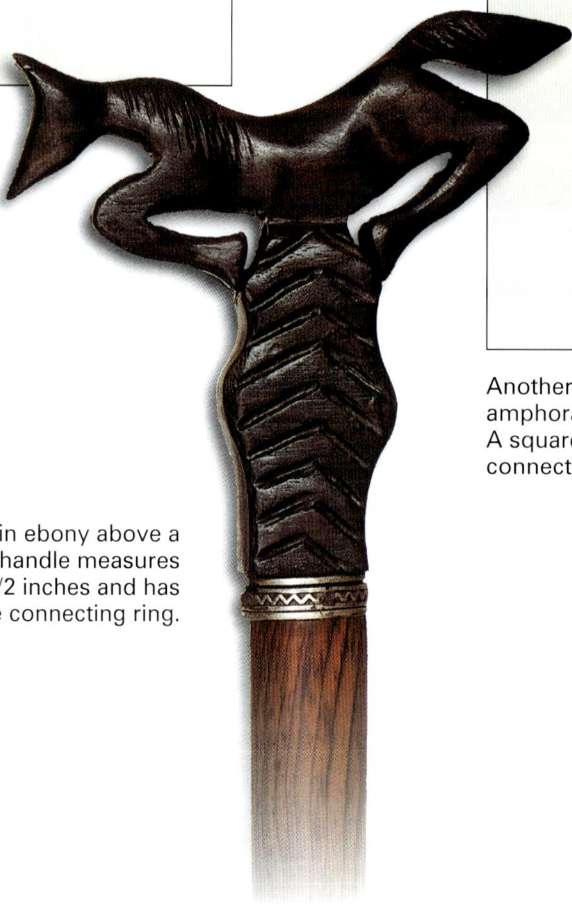

A horse in ebony above a vase. The handle measures 4 1/2 x 4 1/2 inches and has a double connecting ring.

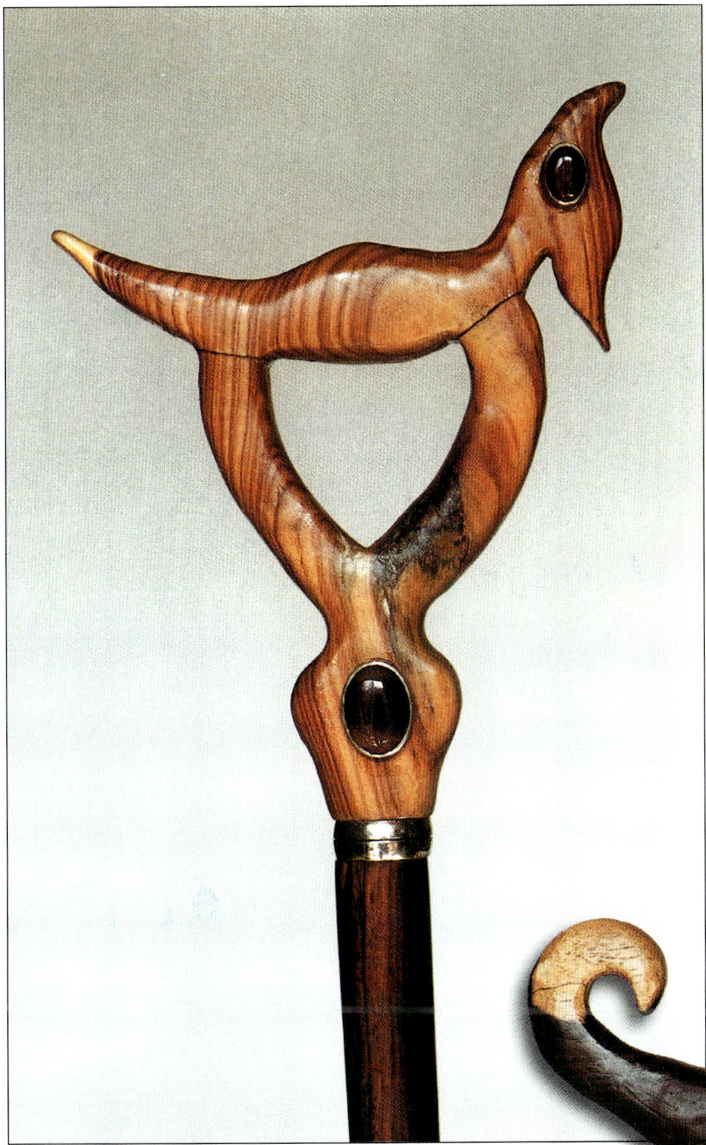

A heart-shaped handle with a bird adorned with two framed amber stones, one for an eye and one is at the base of the tulipwood handle. The handle measures 7 x 5 1/2 inches and has a double silver ring.

Abstract of a bird in Honduras rosewood. The handle measures 6 3/4 x 4 1/2 inches and has a corrugated copper collar.

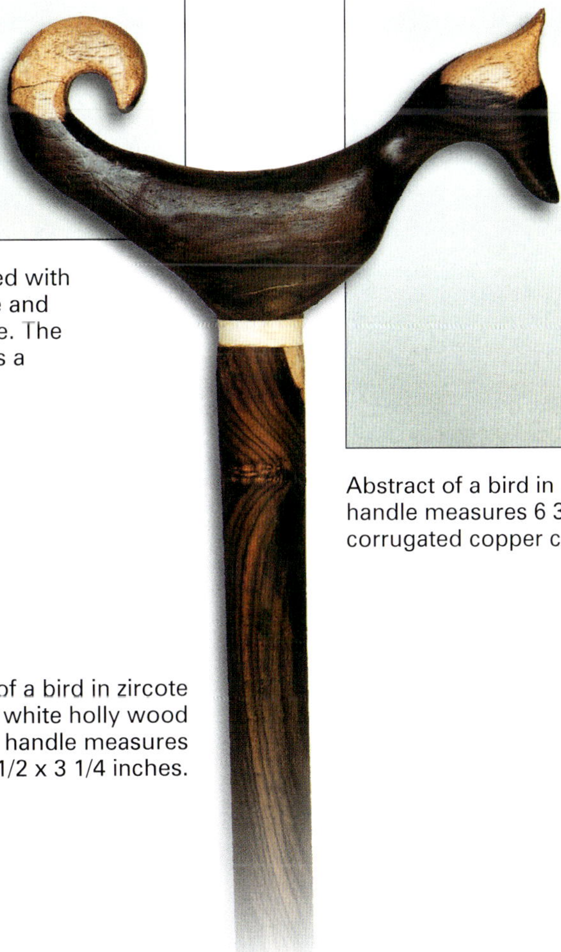

Abstract of a bird in zircote wood with a white holly wood collar. The handle measures 6 1/2 x 3 1/4 inches.

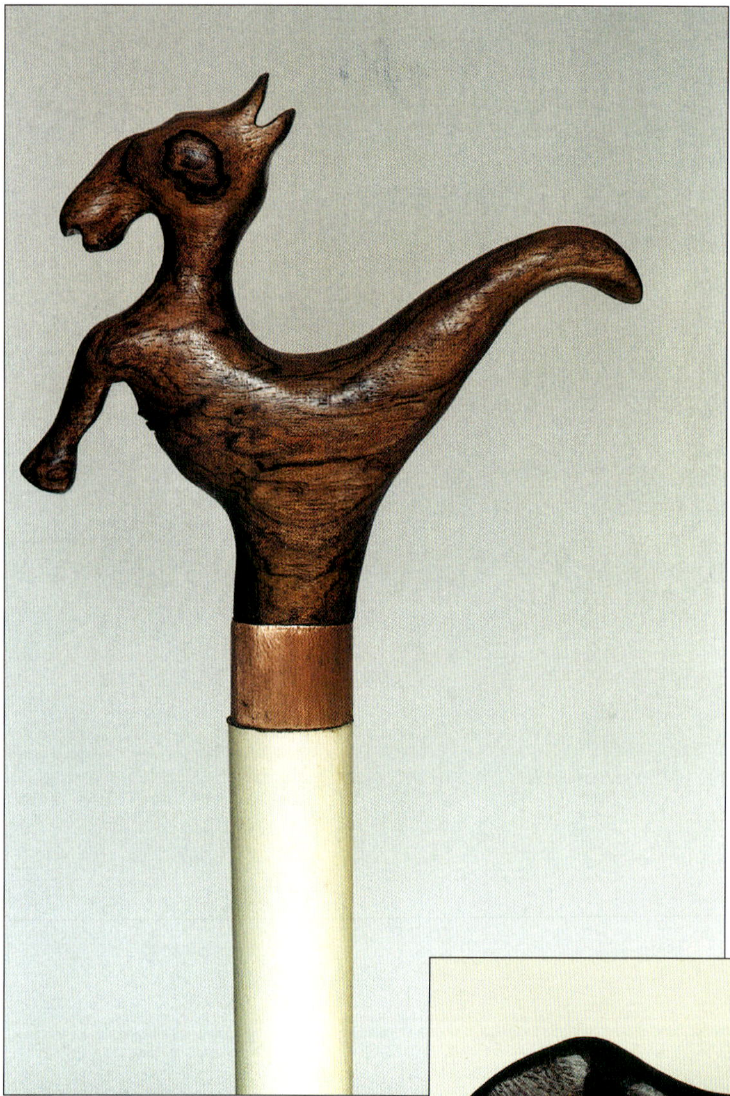

Abstract of a prehistoric animal in Honduras rosewood. The handle measures 5 x 4 inches and has a corrugated copper collar. The shaft is painted white.

Abstract of a seahorse in Macassar ebony with a pearl in one eye and a mounted mother of pearl stone at the base of the sculpture. The handle measures 6 x 4 1/2 inches and has a silver collar.

Abstract of a bird in zircote wood. The collar is in holly wood.

A bird in Macassar ebony. The handle measures 5 1/2 x 3 inches and has a silver collar.

A bird in Honduras rosewood. The handle measures 6 1/2 x 4 1/2 inches and has a corrugated copper collar.

A bird in Macassar ebony. The handle measures 5 x 3 inches and has a silver ring collar.

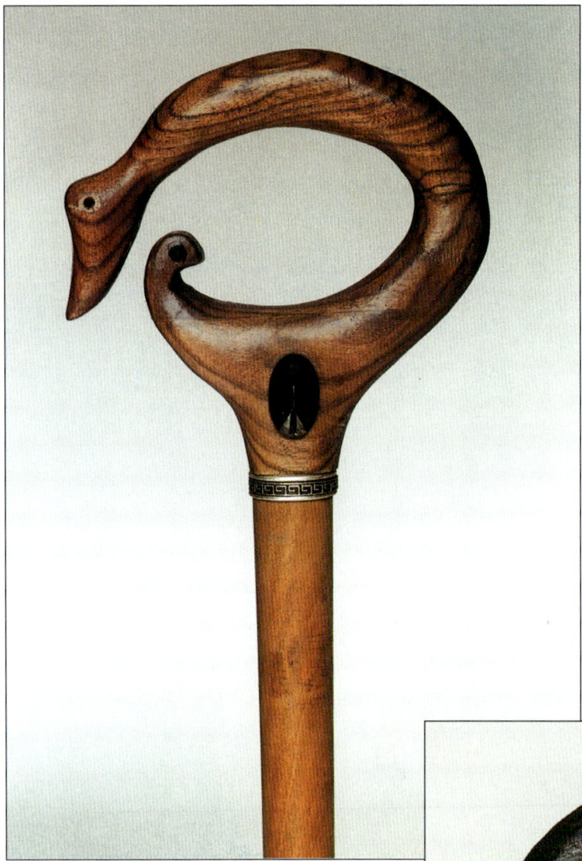

A serpent in a circular mode in Honduras rosewood with a 1 x 1 1/2 inch unframed black stone inserted at the base. The handle measures 5 x 5 inches and has a double silver ring.

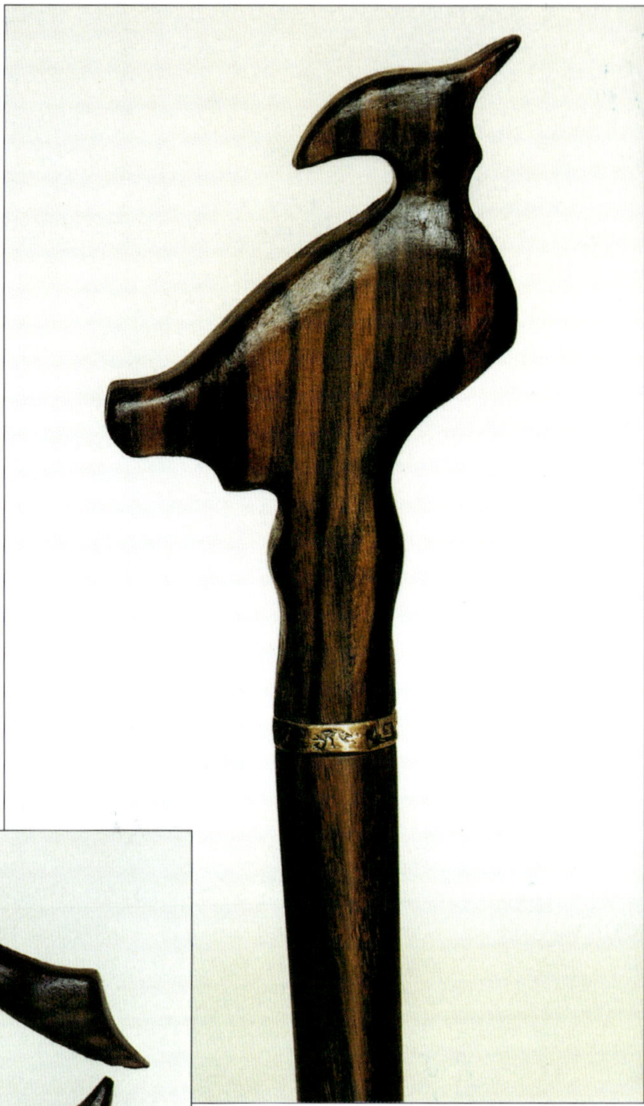

A bird in Macassar ebony. The handle measures 5 x 4 1/2 and has a silver collar.

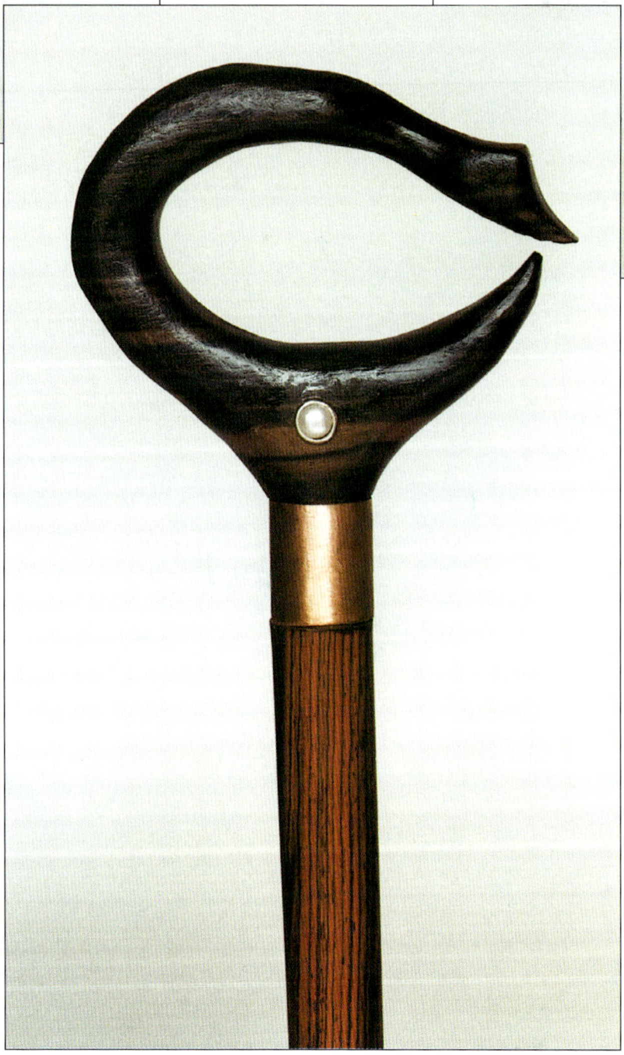

A serpent in a circular shape in Macassar ebony with a pearl attached to the base. The handle measures 4 1/2 x 4 inches and has a corrugated brass collar.

A bird in purple heart wood with a custom-made pendant with small rubies at the base. The handle measures 4 x 4 inches and has a white collar made with holly wood.

A serpent in circular shape in Macassar ebony. A pearl is in the eye with a custom-made pendant with ruby at the base. The handle measures 5 x 5 inches and has a corrugated brass collar.

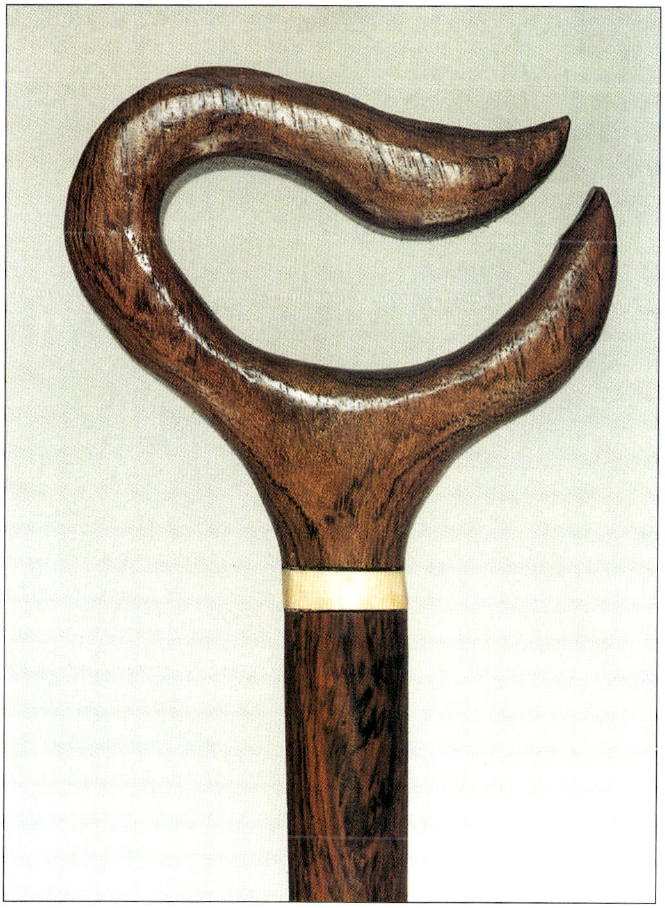

A semicircular handle in rosewood. The handle measures 4 1/2 x 4 inches and has a holly wood collar.

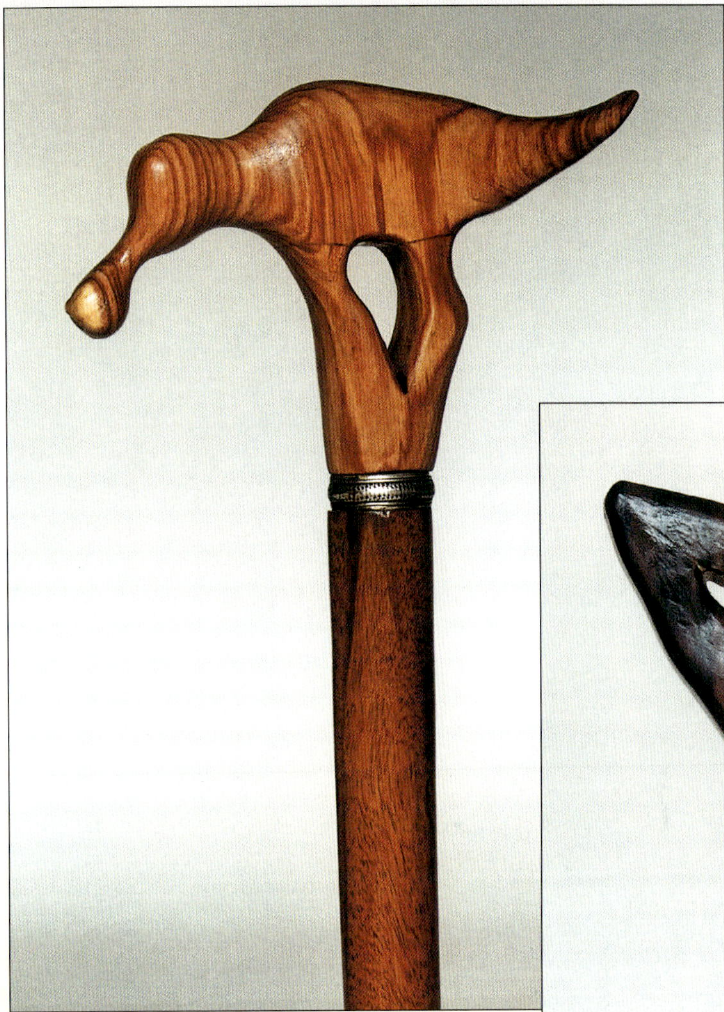

A Rosead Teaspoon Bill bird in tulipwood. The handle measures 5 1/2 x 3 1/2 inches and has a double silver ring.

A bird in Macassar ebony with a lip-type handle for the wings and a silver collar.

Handles In Colorplay™ Wood Made With a Mini-Lathe

Knob-type handle in Ebony Swirl Colorplay adorned with a gemstone without a mount and a mounted amber stone on top. The handle measures 6 x 1 3/4 inches and has a silver collar.

Handle in Ebony Swirl Colorplay adorned with a mounted black onyx stone on top. The handle measures 6 x 2 inches and has a silver collar.

A knob-type handle in Eclipse Colorplay adorned with a holly wood ring with small black stones. The handle measures 6 x 2 inches and has a silver collar.

Knob-type handle in Eclipse Colorplay and holly wood decorated on top with a white pearl. The handle measures 6 x 2 inches and has a silver collar.

Knob-type handle in Patriot Colorplay wood ornamented with a pearl and an amber stone on top. The handle measures 6 x 2 inches and has a silver collar.

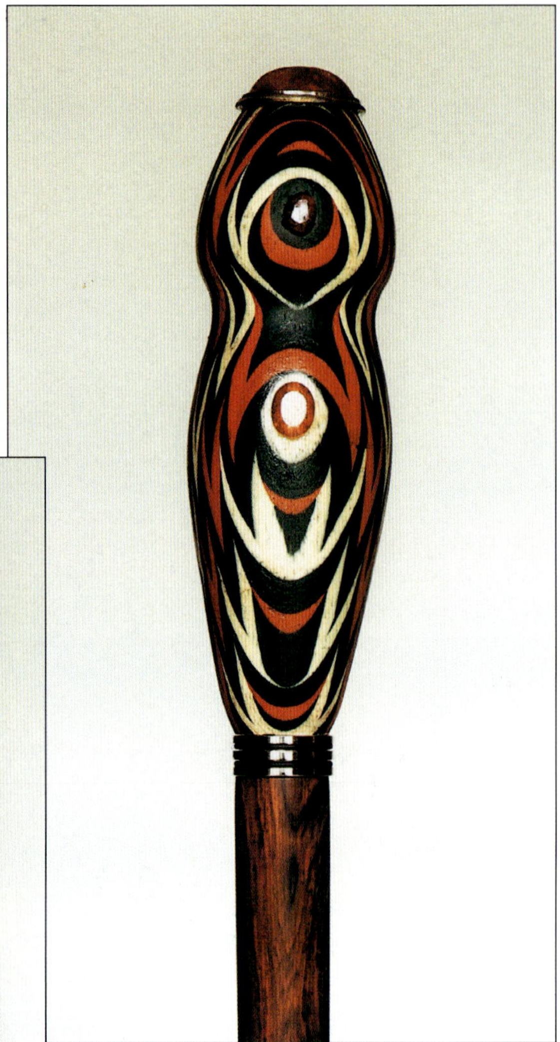

Knob-type handle in Italia Colorplay wood decorated with a gemstone and a mounted amber stone on top. The handle measures 6 x 2 inches and has a silver collar.

Knob-type handle in Italia Colorplay wood decorated with a blue stone on top. The handle measures 6 x 2 inches and has a silver collar.

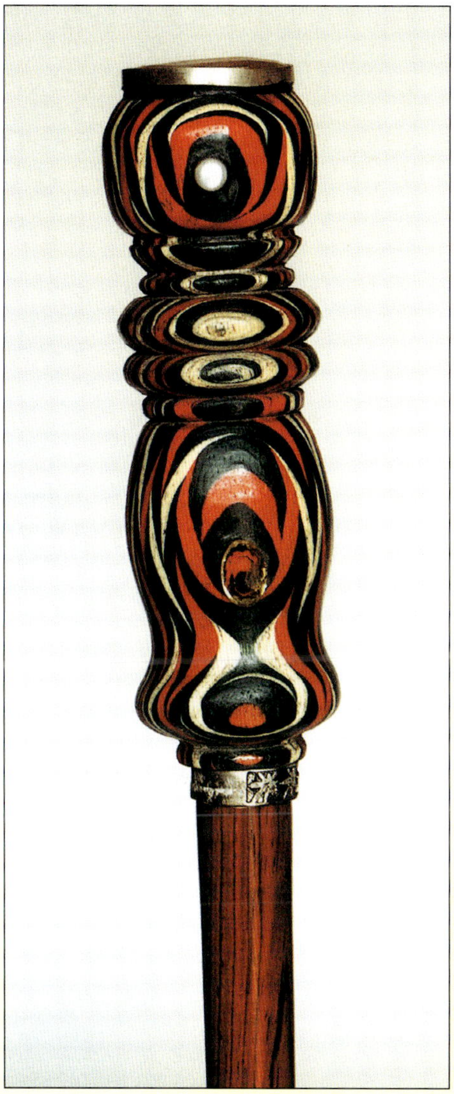

Knob-type handle in Italia Colorplay wood decorated with a pearl and a hard stone on top; the handle measures 6 x 2 inches and has a silver collar.

Knob-type handle in Scarlet Colorplay wood decorated with an amber gemstone on top; the handle measures 3 x 2 1/2 inches and has a silver collar.

Knob-type handle in Eclipse Colorplay wood decorated with a ruby gemstone and a mounted green pendant on top; the handle measures 6 x 2 inches and has a silver collar.

A elliptical shaped handle in ebony decorated with an pink gemstone without a mount and a framed, black onyx stone on top; the handle measures 6 x 2 1/2 inches and has a silver collar.

Handles with Flowers and Corals

Eleven handles with floral motifs featuring insertions of custom-made red and pink corals. All of these handles also include custom-made gold rings.

Handle in zircote wood ornamented with an original mini-sculpture of the Madonna and Child in pink coral surrounded by four roses in pink coral. The connecting ring is in 18 karat solid gold. The handle measures 10 x 6 inches.

The same handle in reverse.

A detail from the Madonna and Child.

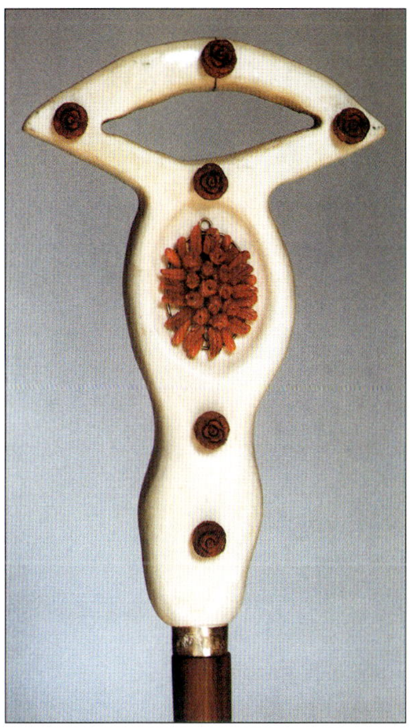

Handle in holly wood ornamented with a bouquet of flowers in red coral and six red roses. The handle measures 9 x 5 1/2 inches and has a gold connecting ring.

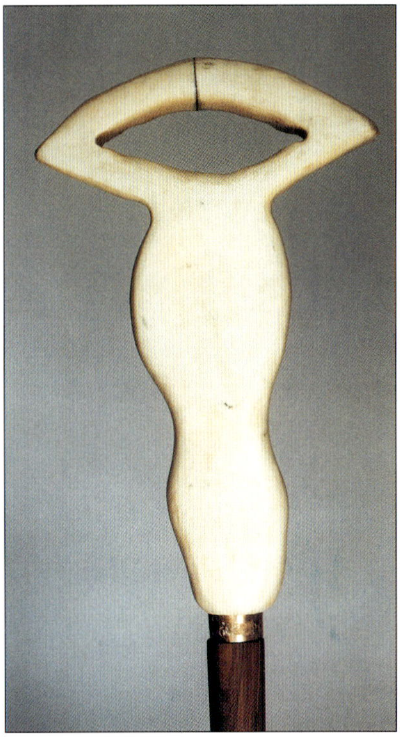

The reverse of the Handle in holly wood ornamented with a bouquet of flowers in red coral and six red roses, (p.55).

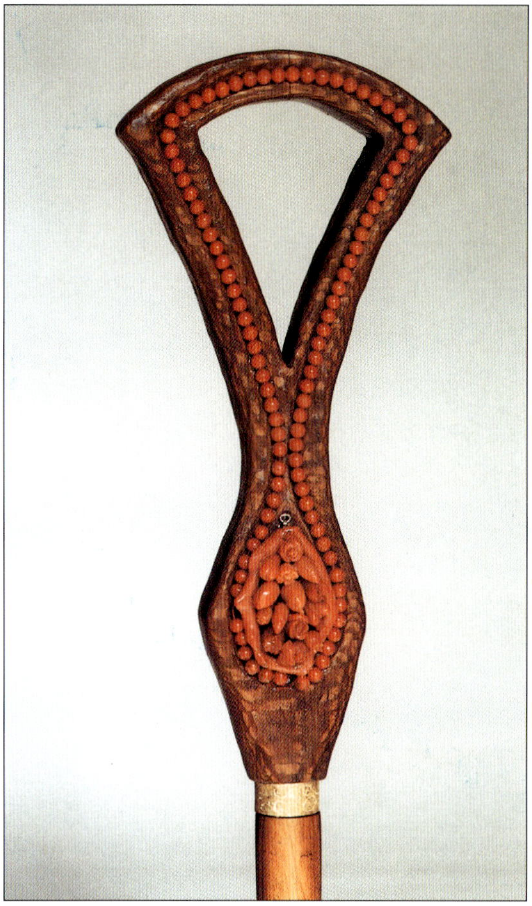

Handle in lacewood ornamented with a collar in red coral and a bouquet of flowers in red coral. The handle measures 10 x 5 inches and has a solid gold connecting ring.

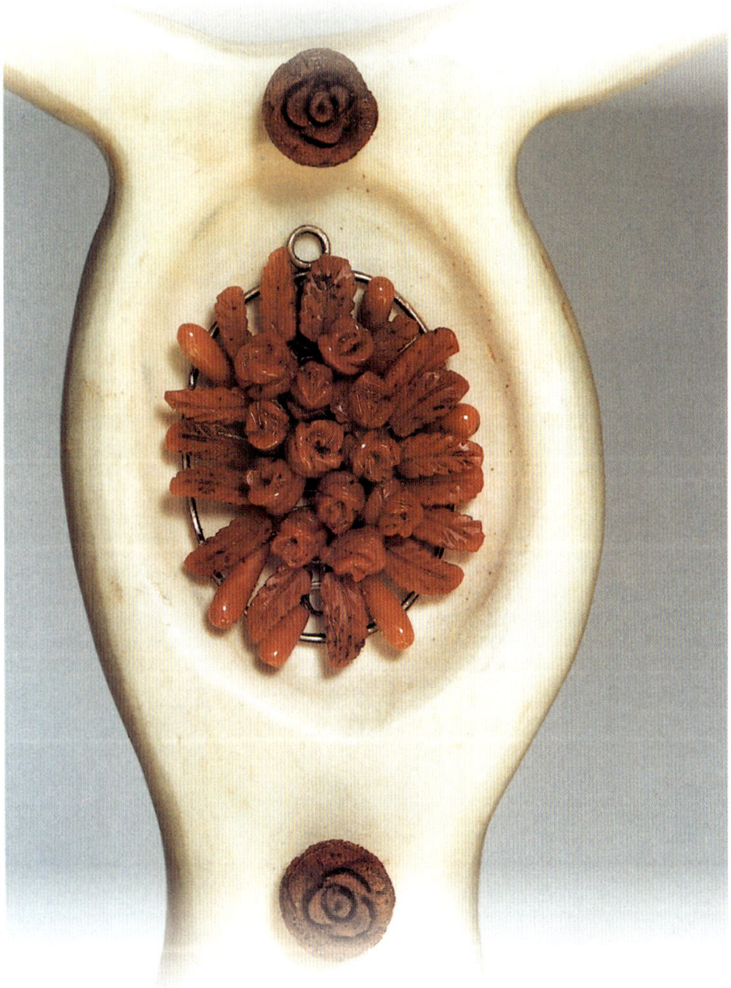

A detail of the bouquet of flowers, (p.55).

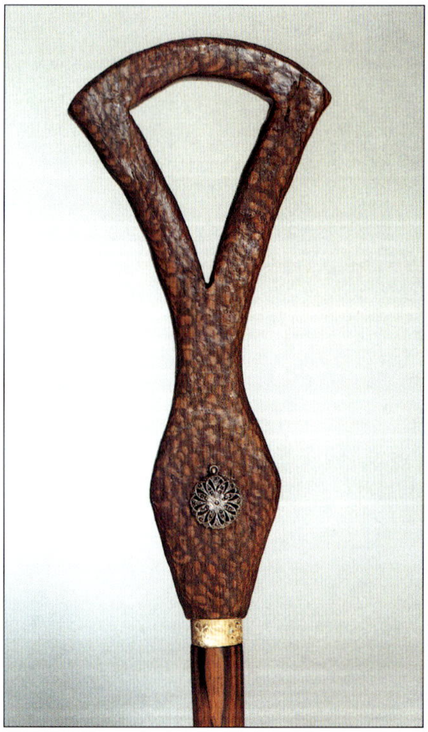

The same handle in reverse with a pendant in silver.

A detail of lacewood and red coral bouquet handle.

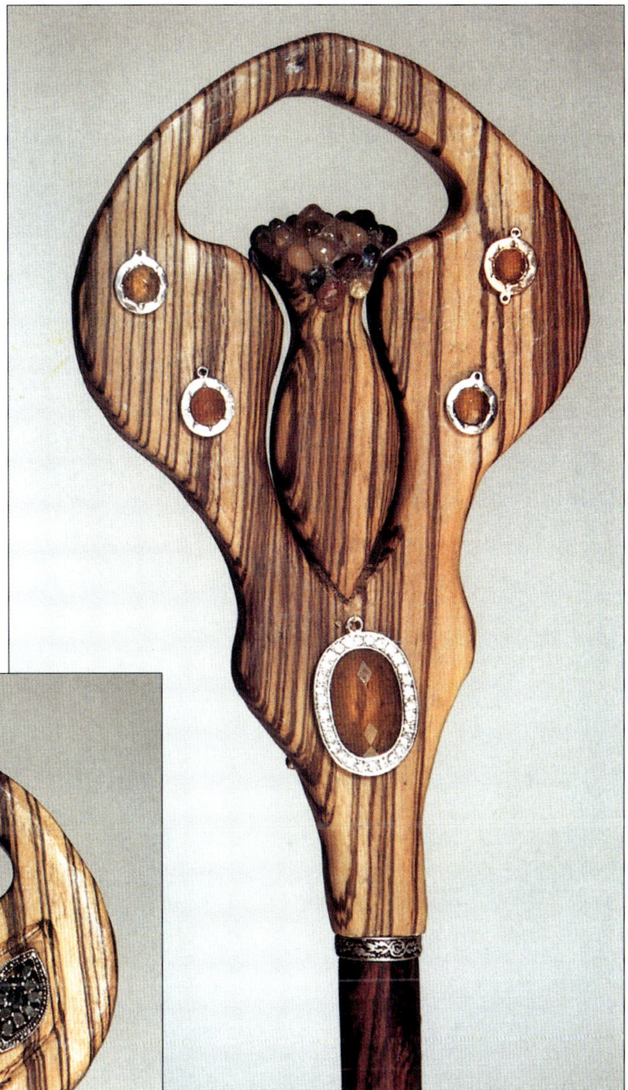

The reverse side of the handle. This side is decorated with five gemstones framed in silver.

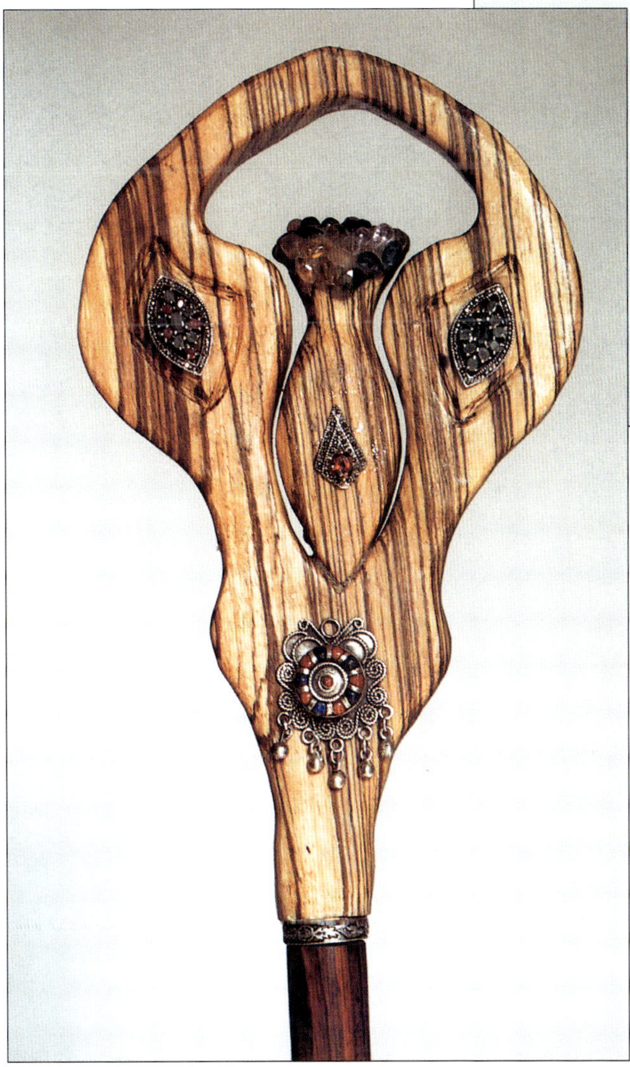

Handle in zebrawood with an amphora at the center. It is ornamented with four different gemstones. The handle measures 10 x 6 inches and has a silver connecting ring.

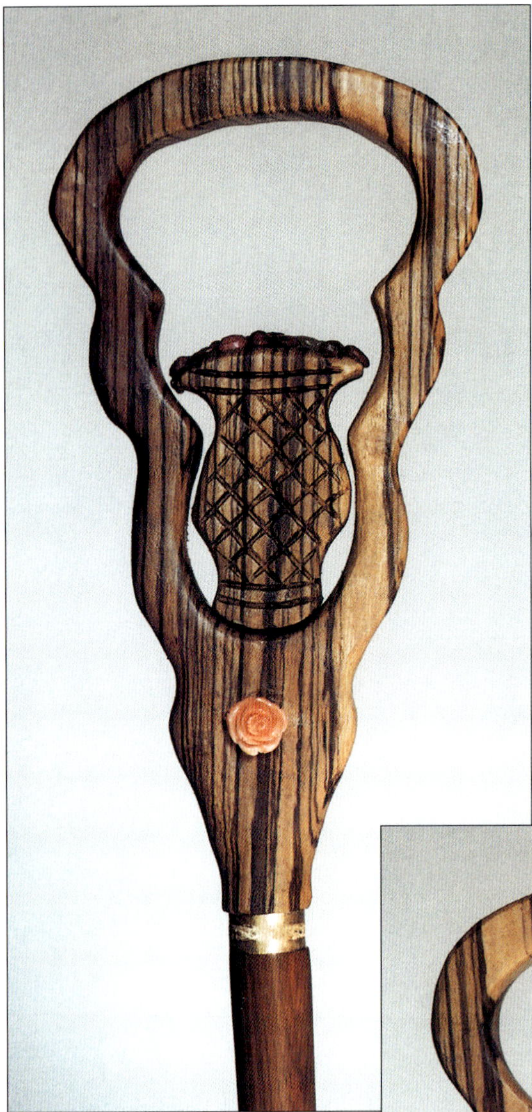

Handle in zebrawood decorated with an amphora and a rose in pink coral. It has a silver connecting ring. The handle measures 10 1/2 x 5 inches.

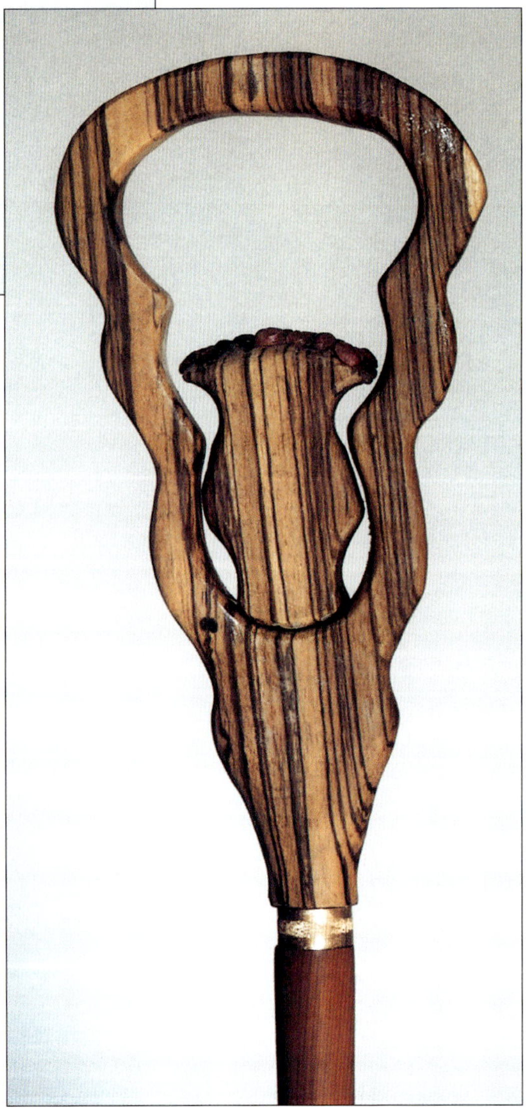

Reverse side of the zebrawood handle.

Handle in tulipwood, the lower deck is an abstract of a flower, has three roses in pink coral at the base. The handle measures 8 1/2 x 5 inches and has a gold connecting ring.

Right:
Reverse side of the tulipwood handle.

Handle in zebrawood: The central flower is in corniola stone with a pink coral rose at the center. Four additional pink coral roses surround the central piece. The handle has a silver connecting ring and measures 9 x 4 1/2 inches.

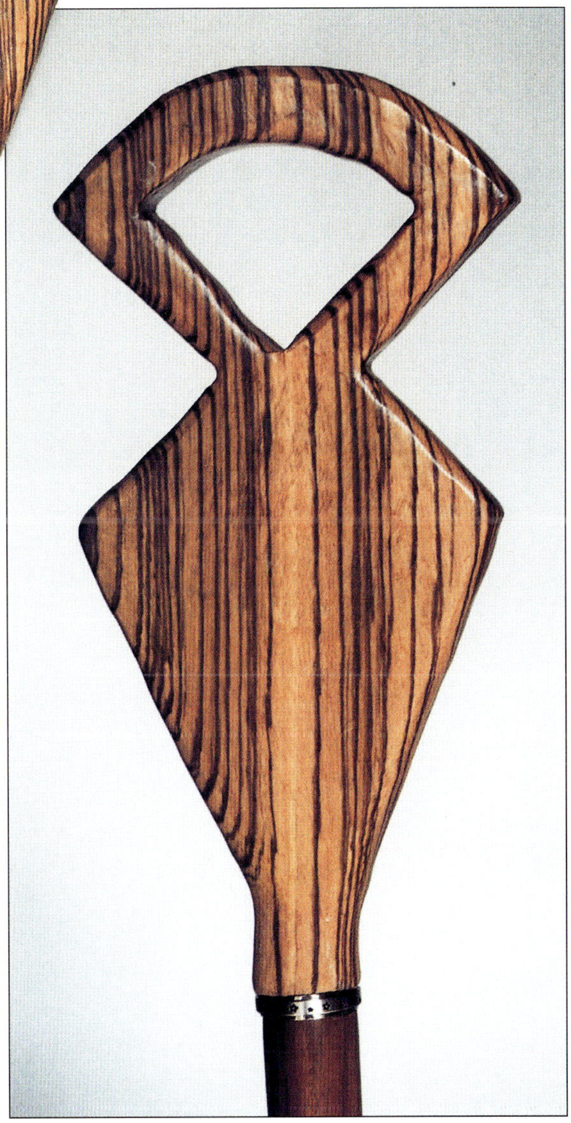

Reverse side of the zebrawood and corniola stone decorated handle.

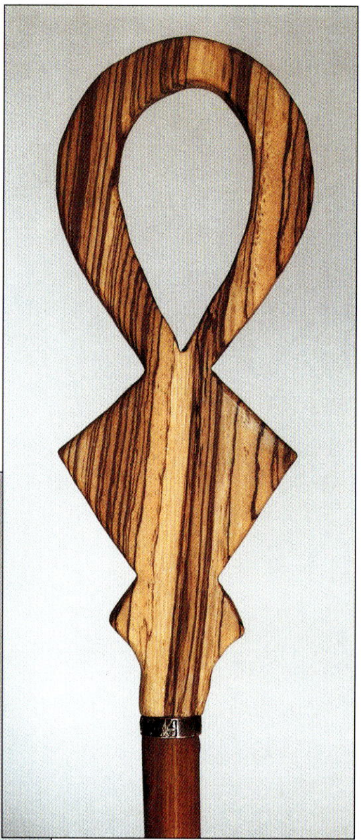

Reverse side of the zebrawood, black gemstone decorated handle.

Handle in zebrawood decorated with mounted and non-mounted black gemstones and a silver connecting ring. The handle measures 11 x 4 1/2 inches.

Double-deck handle in zebrawood: The lower deck is an abstract of a flower with a pink coral rose in the center. A red stone and ten silver balls decorate the rest of the handle. The handle measures 9 1/2 x 4 1/2 inches and has a silver connecting ring.

Reverse side of the double-deck zebrawood handle.

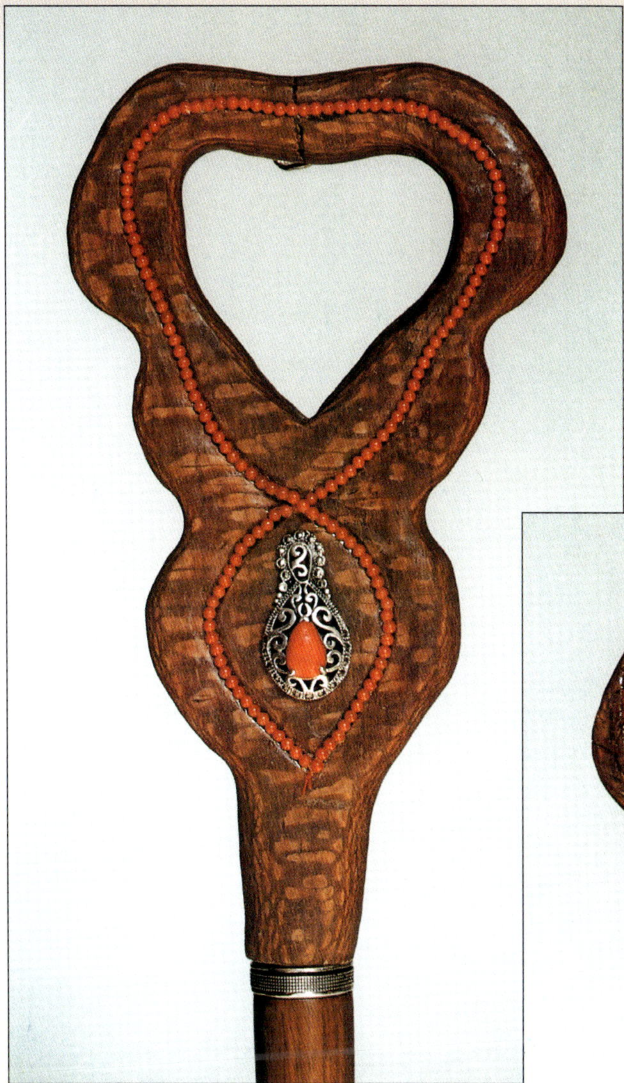

Handle in lacewood with a mounted red stone surrounded by a red coral collar. The handle measures 8 1/2 x 5 inches and has a silver connecting ring.

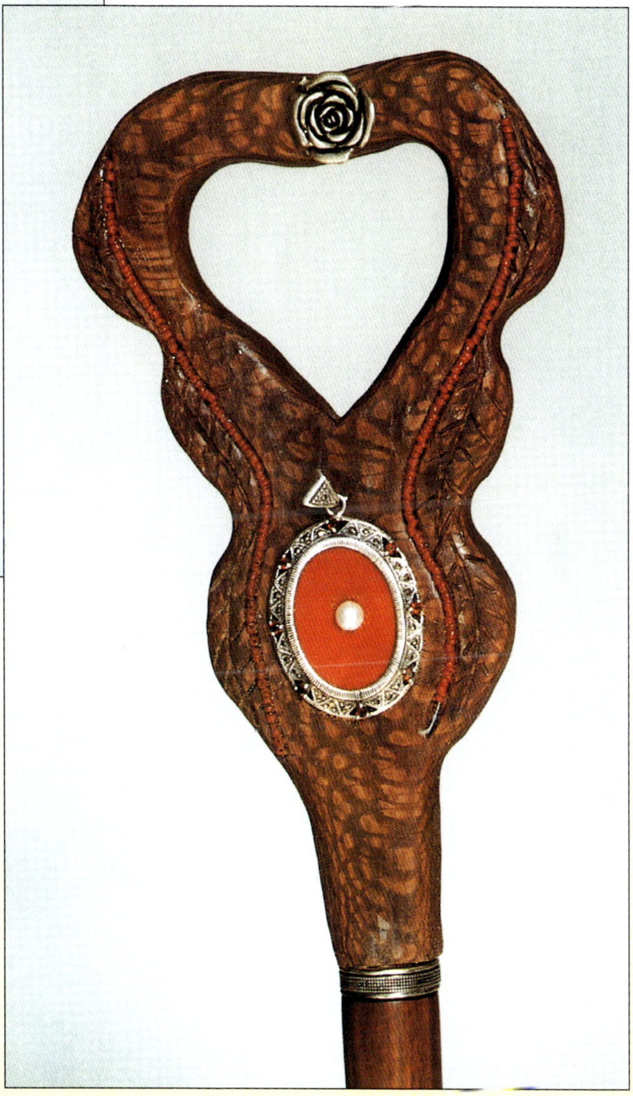

Reverse side of the lacewood handle. A silver rose and a red pendant surrounded by a coral collar decorate this side.

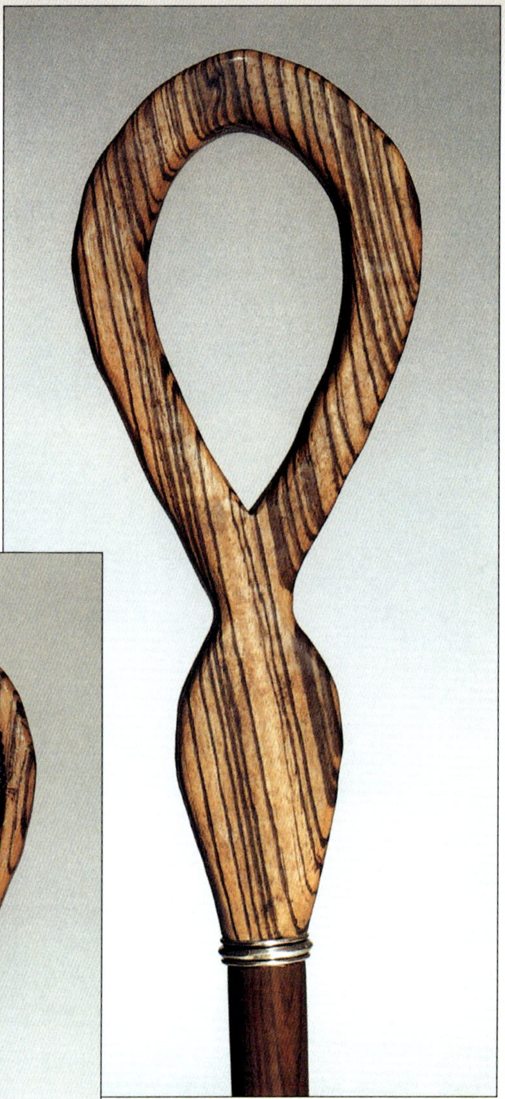

Reverse of zebrawood with mounted violet stone handle.

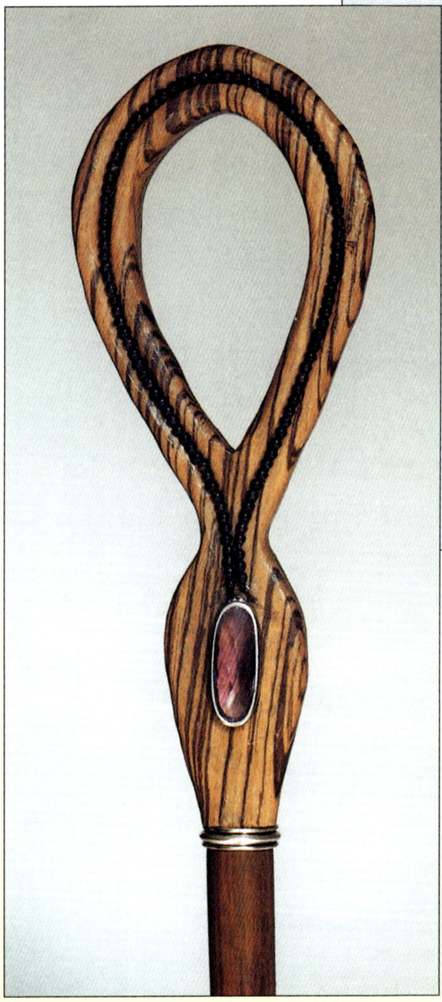

Handle in zebrawood with a mounted violet stone at the base of the handle. A collar of violet stones adorns the handle. The handle measures 10 1/2 x 5 inches and has a silver connecting ring.

Cane Holders

Cane holder in stained mahogany for twenty canes.

Cane holder in natural mahogany in two levels for forty canes.

Cane holder in natural mahogany for thirty canes.

Cane holder, floor type, in stained mahogany for eighteen canes.

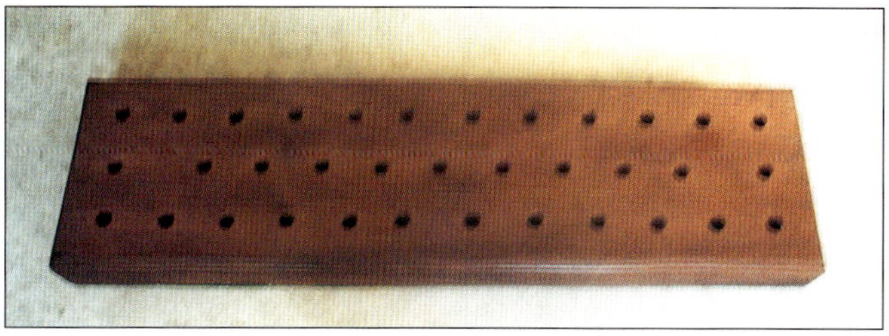

Floor model in walnut for thirty-five canes.

Small floor model in walnut for five canes.

Holders with canes.